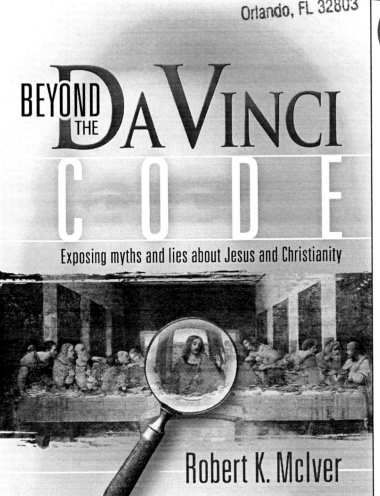

BEYOND THE DAVINCI CODE

Exposing myths and lies about Jesus and Christianity

Robert K. McIver

Pacific Press® Publishing Association

Nampa, Idaho
Oshawa, Ontario, Canada
www.pacificpress.com

PS
3552
.R685
D385
2006

Designed by Gerald Lee Monks

Copyright © 2006 by
Pacific Press® Publishing Association
Printed in the United States of America
All rights reserved

ISBN 13: 978-0-8163-2170-4
ISBN 10: 0-8163-2170-1

Additional copies of this book are available by calling toll free
1-800-765-6955
or by visiting <www.adventistbookcenter.com>

Acknowledgments

Earlier versions of some of the materials in this book have already appeared in print, and I would like to thank *Ministry* magazine and the United States *Signs of the Times*® for permission to use this material. The published articles are *"The Da Vinci Code* and the Nag Hammadi Gospels" on pages 20 and 21 of the May 2006 issue of *Ministry,* "Jesus and *The Da Vinci Code"* on pages 8, 9, and 13 of the May 2006 issue of *Signs of the Times*®, and *"The Da Vinci Code* and the Christian Day of Worship," on pages 26, 27, and 29 of the October 2006 issue of *Signs of the Times*®.

TABLE OF CONTENTS

CHAPTER 1 | The Conspiracy

You may be one of the millions worldwide who have read Dan Brown's runaway bestseller, *The Da Vinci Code.* Or you may have seen Hollywood's recent movie version. But even if you haven't read the book or seen the movie, it's unlikely that you have been able to escape all the media attention—and controversy—focused on this publishing sensation.

After spending record amounts of time on the top-ten bestseller lists prior to the movie release, sales of *The Da Vinci Code* finally slowed to the extent that the book slipped from the lists. This, mind you, after it had sold more than forty million copies and had been translated into forty-four languages.[1] Then came the movie. Although it received very mixed reviews, the movie, starring Tom Hanks and Audrey Tautou, had the distinction of being the "second biggest [movie] opening weekend of all time worldwide."[2] By July 11, while still showing in theatres, the movie had moved to twenty-second place on the all time worldwide box-office figures for movies, the most successful movie by far in the first six months of 2006.[3] And as these words are written in mid-July 2006, the print version of *The Da Vinci Code* is back in the top-ten bestseller lists! Presumably, enough people who saw the movie without reading the book are now curious to know what the book itself is like. *The Da Vinci Code* continues to break all records. The media are going to have to find new words to describe its success: "Bestseller" or "Number One Bestseller" appears too ordinary. Perhaps it should be called a "Mega-Blockbuster Bestseller"!

Why has a work of fiction caused such a stir?

The Da Vinci Code is a potent mix of conspiracy, danger, religiously motived murder, mysterious symbols, and puzzles—with even a touch of sex as part of religious ritual. But most of all, it is about an astonishing religious conspiracy. At the heart of its plot is the claim that much about the beginnings of the Christian church and Jesus' role in Christianity are not at all what the church and Christians have presented them to be. According to this conspiracy theory, the Roman emperor Constantine radically changed Christianity in the fourth century A.D., suppressing "authentic" elements of Christianity to suit his political needs. In fact, *The Da Vinci Code* argues that Christianity is really nothing more than a giant conspiracy that goes back to Constantine rather than to Jesus.

Is this true? That's what we will examine in this book.

Of course, there are all kinds of claims about Christianity floating around today, but those in *The Da Vinci Code* have gained so much attention because they are embedded in a story that has fascinated millions—and because they are presented in the book as plausible historical fact.

The Da Vinci Code, both book and movie, puts forward a series of intriguing clues and "proofs" to make the conspiracy theory sound believable. Readers and viewers who enter into the narrative world where the theory is accepted as true find the book and movie very exciting. Afterward, though, the question naturally arises, "How much of the conspiracy theory is true in real life, not just in books and movies?" Most people have vague memories of hearing about Constantine and the important role he played in the development of Christianity. Many have also heard something about the discoveries of gospel accounts not included in our Bible. So they think that there is a possibility that the ideas in *The Da Vinci Code* might be true, but they are not sure.

This book you hold in your hands will present the evidence for Constantine's involvement in Christian history and assess his impact on the Christian church. Unlike *The Da Vinci Code,* we will not weave a mixture of fiction, conjecture, and half-truths—and call it reality. We will deal in historical facts and biblical evidence. As well as looking at Constantine, we will also need to talk about a number of other things along the way, such as the gospels written in the early centuries of Christianity that didn't make it into the Christian part of the Bible, the New Testament. We will ask the question, Who decided what writings should be in the New Testament? We will look at the claim made in *The Da Vinci Code* that Constantine even changed what Christians thought about the nature of Jesus and the Christian day of worship. But first, let us look at what *The Da Vinci Code* characters say about Constantine's role in the formation of Christianity.

The story thus far . . .

The Da Vinci Code begins with a murder. Jacques Saunièr, curator at the Louvre museum in Paris, is mortally wounded by a pistol shot from a tall, albino attacker. He has managed to set off the security barriers to prevent the murderer from getting any closer to him, but the same barriers that keep the attacker at bay also imprison him. He knows he has only minutes to live. During those minutes he must pass on a terrible secret to somebody he trusts, but how? When his body is finally discovered, it is surrounded by cryptic clues.

Soon, the main characters arrive on the scene: Sophie Neveu and Robert Langdon. An expert in codes and ciphers working for the Parisian police, Sophie, it turns out, is also the granddaughter of the murdered curator. Langdon, a consultant called by the police, is a professor of religious symbology at Harvard University. Warned by Sophie, Langdon gradually realizes that he is not really acting as a consultant for the police but is in fact their main suspect. Together, Langdon and Sophie solve the first clues left by Saunièr and escape from the Louvre. To clear his name, Langdon must not only stay free but also work with Sophie to solve the mystery that lies behind Saunièr's murder. For the rest of the book, the two heroes stay just ahead of the police and the murderer, Silas—and the powerful religious authorities who control him.

The first set of clues leads our heroes to a bank vault from which they recover a small polished rosewood box with a hand-carved inlay of a five-petaled rose. Langdon immediately recognizes the rose as a symbol of the Holy Grail, the cup from which Jesus drank wine with His disciples at the Last Supper just before His crucifixion. It briefly passes through Langdon's mind that perhaps the box might contain the Holy Grail itself. But no, they find in the box a complex cylinder made of polished marble that includes five disks, each labelled with an entire alphabet. Sophie recognizes it as a cryptex, invented by Leonardo da Vinci as a special way to store secrets. In a cryptex, the secret is written on a thin sheet of papyrus, a type of ancient paper, and wrapped around a delicate glass vial filled with vinegar. Someone who has the password is able to open the cryptex and recover the secret message. But if force is used, the vinegar container would break and the vinegar would dissolve the papyrus before anyone could read its secrets.

Langdon then realizes that although what they are holding is not the Grail itself, it *is* the fabled keystone, said to contain the secret of the location of the Holy Grail. But how to open the cryptex? They need help and a place to hide. Langdon immediately thinks of the noted Grail expert and former British Royal Historian, Sir Leigh Teabing, who is currently residing not far from Paris. Sophie and Langdon show up at his home and are admitted, and Teabing's servant provides tea and scones—a welcome respite from the tension of the last few hours. While they talk, the shape of the conspiracy that goes back to Emperor Constantine emerges.

The British Royal Historian, Sir Leigh Teabing

Sophie, it turns out, knows next to nothing about the Holy Grail. Between them, Langdon and Teabing set about informing her that the Grail is not, in fact, the cup of Christ; it is a person. They begin by telling her about the Bible and Emperor Constantine's role in its formation and in establishing that Jesus was divine: Let's let them tell it in their own words.[4]

"But first we must speak of the Bible." Teabing smiled. "And everything you need to know about the Bible can be summed up by the great canon doctor Martyn Percy." Teabing cleared his throat and declared, "The Bible did not arrive by fax from heaven."

"I beg your pardon?"

"The Bible is a product of *man,* my dear. Not of God. The Bible did not fall magically from the clouds. . . .

"Jesus Christ was a historical figure of staggering influence, perhaps the most enigmatic and inspirational leader the world has ever seen. . . . Understandably, His life was recorded by thousands of followers across the land." Teabing paused to sip his tea and then placed the cup back on the mantel. "More than *eighty* gospels were considered for the New Testament, and yet only a relative few were chosen for inclusion—Matthew, Mark, Luke, and John among them."

"Who chose which gospels to include?" Sophie asked.

"Aha!" Teabing burst in with enthusiasm. "The fundamental irony of Christianity! The Bible, as we know it today, was collated by the pagan Roman emperor Constantine the Great."

"I thought Constantine was a Christian," Sophie said.

"Hardly," Teabing scoffed. "He was a lifelong pagan who was baptized on his deathbed, too weak to protest."[5]

Teabing and Langdon explain that Constantine was the head priest of Rome's official religion of sun worship. Yet even so, because he saw that Christianity was on the rise, he "backed the winning horse." He did so, says Teabing, "by fusing pagan symbols, dates, and rituals into the growing Christian tradition." Teabing and Langdon give a number of examples of this fusion: The halos seen on icons of Christian saints are actually Egyptian sun disks; the symbols of the miter, the altar, and the Communion are taken from "pagan mystery religions." Teabing goes on to say,

"By the way, December 25 is also the birthday of Osiris, Adonis, and Dionysus. . . . Even Christianity's weekly holy day was stolen from the pagans."

"What do you mean?"

"Originally," Langdon said, "Christianity honored the Jewish Sabbath of Saturday, but Constantine shifted it to coincide with the pagan's veneration day of the sun." He paused, grinning. "To this day, most churchgoers attend services on Sunday morning with no idea that they are there on account of the pagan sun god's weekly tribute—*Sun*day."

Sophie's head was spinning. "And all of this relates to the Grail?"

"Indeed," Teabing said. "Stay with me. During this fusion of religions, Constantine needed to strengthen the new Christian tradition, and held a famous ecumenical gathering known as the Council of Nicaea."

Sophie had heard of it only insofar as its being the birthplace of the Nicene Creed.

"At this gathering," Teabing said, "many aspects of Christianity were debated and voted upon—the date of Easter, the role of the bishops, the administration of sacraments, and, of course, the *divinity* of Jesus."

"I don't follow. His divinity?"

"My dear," Teabing declared, "until *that* moment in history, Jesus was viewed by His followers as a mortal prophet . . . a great and powerful man, but a *man* nonetheless. A mortal."

"Not the Son of God?"

"Right," Teabing said. "Jesus' establishment as 'the Son of God' was officially proposed and voted on by the Council of Nicaea."

"Hold on. You're saying Jesus' divinity was the result of a *vote?*"

"A relatively close vote at that," Teabing added.[6]

Teabing then explains that by declaring Jesus divine, Constantine created "an entity whose power was unchallengeable. . . .

"It was all about power." He further explains that the publication of the Bible was one of Constantine's most important steps:

"The twist is this," Teabing said, talking faster now. "Because Constantine upgraded Jesus' status almost four centuries *after* Jesus' death, thousands of documents already existed chronicling His life as a *mortal* man. To rewrite the history books, Constantine knew he would need a bold stroke. From this sprang the most profound moment in Christian history." Teabing paused, eyeing Sophie. "Constantine commissioned and financed a new Bible, which omitted those gospels that spoke of Christ's *human* traits and embellished those gospels that made Him godlike. The earlier gospels were outlawed, gathered up, and burned. . . ."

"Fortunately for historians," Teabing said, "some of the gospels that Constantine attempted to eradicate managed to survive. The Dead Sea Scrolls were found in the 1950s hidden in a cave near Qumran in the Judaean desert. And, of course, the Coptic Scrolls in 1945 at Nag Hammadi. In addition to telling the true Grail story, these documents speak of Christ's ministry in very human terms."[7]

Toward the end of chapter 55 and through chapters 56 and 58, the discussion finally returns to the question of the Holy Grail and the paintings of Leonardo da Vinci. According to Teabing, da Vinci's painting of the Last Supper in fact reveals several things about the Holy Grail. In it one can see that each person at the table has his own cup—there was not one common chalice or Grail. The Grail was not the cup, but a person. In fact, "the Holy Grail is a woman."[8] In da Vinci's painting of the Last Supper we can see that this woman, quite unexpectedly, is right there sitting down with the other disciples at the supper.

Langdon smiled. "As it turns out, the Holy Grail *does* indeed make an appearance in *The Last Supper*. Leonardo included her prominently."

"Hold on," Sophie said. "You told me the Holy Grail is a *woman*. *The Last Supper* is a painting of thirteen men."

"Is it?" Teabing arched his eyebrows. "Take a closer look."

Uncertain, Sophie made her way closer to the painting, scanning the thirteen figures—Jesus Christ in the middle, six disciples on His left, and six on His right. "They're all men," she confirmed.

"Oh?" Teabing said. "How about the one seated in the place of honor, at the right hand of the Lord?"

Sophie examined the figure to Jesus' immediate right, focusing in. As she studied the person's face and body, a wave of astonishment rose within her. The individual had flowing red hair, delicate folded hands, and the hint of a bosom. It was, without a doubt . . . female.

"That's a woman!" Sophie exclaimed.

Teabing was laughing. "Surprise, surprise. Believe me, it's no mistake. Leonardo was skilled at painting the difference between the sexes."

Sophie could not take her eyes from the woman beside Christ. *The Last Supper is supposed* to *be thirteen men. Who is this woman?*[9]

By the way, the cover of the book you are reading includes a clear view of the individual sitting next to Jesus in da Vinci's painting—usually thought to be the disciple John. You can glance at the cover to see whether you, too, can see "a hint of a bosom." I must confess, I looked with some interest at a reproduction of the fresco but found myself unconvinced that the person seated on Jesus' right was a woman. But you can decide for yourself.

Sophie, on the other hand, *was* convinced that da Vinci had painted a woman in that place of importance. The rest of chapter 58 of *The Da Vinci Code* reveals that the "woman" sitting beside Jesus was none other than Mary Magdalene. Not only this, Langdon and Teabing insist she was married to Jesus, was pregnant at the time of the Crucifixion, and subsequently gave birth to a daughter. In another chapter we will look more carefully at the evidence they give to support their claims about the relationship between Mary Magdalene and Jesus. But the broad outline of the conspiracy theory Dan Brown puts forward in *The Da Vinci Code* is now clear enough.

The conspiracy

Chapters 55, 56, and 58 of *The Da Vinci Code* contain a concise explanation of what the book claims are the real origins of Christianity:

- Christianity as it is known today does not, in fact, go back to Jesus, but goes back to Emperor Constantine.
- Constantine actively suppressed certain important features of Christianity that celebrated the role of the sacred feminine element.
- He suppressed early gospels that highlighted the role of Mary Magdalene and chose, instead, those that elevated the role of the male.
- In doing so, he radically changed Christianity from what it had been.

The Da Vinci Code is a work of fiction, and one might fairly ask whether the author, Dan Brown, actually believes that Christianity as it is known today is but the results of a conspiracy that goes back to Emperor Constantine. Some evidence suggests that he does.[10] Certainly, the book itself carries enough plausibility to alarm many Christians.[11] That it was roundly condemned by several prominent Catholic bishops did not hurt its sales, and that Rowan Williams, archbishop of Canterbury and head of the Anglican Church, took opportunity in his widely quoted 2006 Easter message to attack the book,[12] was no doubt viewed by the publisher of *The Da Vinci Code* as wonderful free advertising.

Many who read the book or viewed the movie came away wondering how much of the book's claims actually correspond to historical fact. What role did Emperor Constantine play in influencing Christianity? Is it true that he suppressed certain gospels that otherwise should have been included in the Bible? Did he change how Christians viewed the divinity of Jesus, and did he change the day of worship?

All of these are fair questions, and we will deal with them one after the other. In fact, it might be a good idea to list in a chart the main claims Dan Brown puts into the mouth of his character Teabing in *The Da Vinci Code*. As we examine the evidence, we can provide a clear response to each of these claims. The claims are listed in the following table:

Constantine's "conspiracy" as alleged by the characters in *The Da Vinci Code*	
Claim by the "Royal Historian," Teabing:	True or False?
"Constantine . . . was a lifelong pagan who was baptized on his deathbed, too weak to protest" (p. 313).	

Claim by the "Royal Historian," Teabing:	True or False?
"By fusing pagan symbols, dates, and rituals into the growing Christian tradition, he created a kind of hybrid religion that was acceptable to both parties" (p. 314).	
"Christianity honored the Jewish Sabbath of Saturday, but Constantine shifted it to coincide with the pagan's veneration day of the sun" (pp. 314, 315).	
"Until that moment in history [the Council of Nicaea], Jesus was viewed by His followers as a mortal prophet . . . a great and powerful man, but a man nonetheless. A mortal" (p. 315).	
"To rewrite the history books, Constantine knew he would need a bold stroke. From this sprang the most profound moment in Christian history. . . . Constantine commissioned and financed a new Bible, which omitted those gospels which spoke of Christ's human traits and embellished those gospels that made Him godlike" (pp. 316, 317).	
"Mary Magdalene was the Holy Vessel. She was the chalice that bore the royal bloodline of Jesus Christ. She was the womb that bore the lineage" (p. 336).	

As we deal with these claims in subsequent chapters, we will be able to fill in the right column of the chart with comments and conclusions based on the biblical and historical evidence. Let's begin, though, by considering Constantine himself, the key player in the conspiracy, according to the characters Teabing and Langdon.

CHAPTER 2

Who Was Constantine and Was He a Lifelong Pagan?

A number of significant historical figures carry the name *Constantine*. But there is little confusion who is usually meant by "Emperor Constantine"—Constantine I (27 February 272–22 May 337), sometimes called Constantine the Great.

Possible evidence that Constantine was a lifelong pagan

The character Teabing describes Constantine as "a lifelong pagan who was baptized on his deathbed, too weak to protest."[1] He supports his assertion by noting that Constantine was the head priest of Rome's official religion of sun worship—the cult of *Sol Invictus*. Though Teabing does not mention it, further evidence for Constantine's pagan status could be cited. For example, until he symbolically relinquished his imperial power on his deathbed, Constantine kept the then-pagan title of *pontifex maximus* that had fallen to him when he was promoted from Caesar to Augustus. Public subsidies of the ancient cults of Rome continued under Constantine, and in fact, long after his death. As *pontifex maximus,* Constantine even appointed new members to the Roman (pagan) priestly colleges. Under his rule, pagan temples in the western half of the empire retained their treasures and endowments and openly celebrated traditional rites.[2] While the best known works that praise Constantine's role as emperor might have been written by Christians, there were some pagans who also wrote praising Constantine's virtues. Thus, a case can be made that Constantine was a pagan.

Yet the reality is most likely somewhat more complicated. Constantine came to power at a complicated time. Nor was it just the religious world that provided difficult challenges. All his adult career, Constantine was a player on a very dangerous and convoluted political stage.

Christianity and Constantine's rise to power

Constantine was born in the year 272, into the household of a successful officer in the Roman army, Constantius Chlorus. When Constantine was about twenty-one years old, his father became Caesar and one of two junior members of a college of four emperors—Diocletian and Maximian, who were titled Augustus, and Constantius and Galerius, who were titled Caesar. Much of the time in the Roman Empire, politics had a lethal aspect, and this was particularly true of politics during this time period. Advancement was sometimes by assassination. Diocletian himself had come to the throne after the mysterious death of his predecessor. So Constantine's position as heir to Constantius was, at the same time, a position of both great opportunity and great danger.

After serving in the east as an army officer, Constantine joined Diocletian's court in 301 or 302, where he was seen as a potential future Caesar or Augustus. A particularly dramatic rearrangement of power took place in 205 when Diocletian announced that he was retiring and that he was appointing two new Caesars—neither of whom was Constantine. As a potential rival of the new Caesars, Constantine's life was in danger. Very sensibly, he quickly made his way to his father's court; his father had by that time been promoted to the rank of Augustus. There is even a story that in his escape, Constantine hamstrung the post horse at each stage stop so that he could stay ahead of any pursuit. Soon after, when Constantine was about thirty-four years old, his father died, and Constantine was saluted as emperor by his father's troops.

Constantine claimed thereafter that his father had declared him his heir, with the rank of Augustus. He was recognized as Caesar by Galerius, who by this time had become the Augustus of the eastern half of the empire. Thus by 306 A.D., Constantine was fairly securely established as Caesar in the territories of Britain and Gaul (a Roman province somewhat equivalent to modern France).

This is when politics and religion intersect in a way that eventually played a role in securing Constantine's supremacy over the whole Roman Empire. In 303 A.D., perhaps at the prompting of Galerius, Diocletian had instigated an empirewide persecution of Christians. This persecution was most severe in the eastern part of the empire and in Africa, where churches were razed, copies of the Bible burned, and many Christians were tortured and put to death. Constantine's father, Constantius, had mitigated its effects in his territories. Constantine went further. As soon as he came to power, he proclaimed a formal end to the persecution of Christians in his domain, restoring to them property they had lost during the time of persecution. From this moment on, then, Constantine portrayed himself as the champion of Christians.

Using a mixture of patience and military force, Constantine first added Italy to his domain in 312 A.D., and the eastern part of the empire by 324 A.D. At this time he became increasingly proactive as a Christian, even taking a significant part in some important decision-making councils of the Christian church, as we will see in a later chapter. In the east, he also raised considerable revenue by sending officials to every city and town, where they sought out the temples and shrines of traditional gods and confiscated anything of value they could find—gold, silver, precious stones, even bronze doors. The temples in the western half of the empire had been allowed to maintain their wealth, but in the east there was a very significant movement of assets from the pagan temples to Constantine, and via his gifts, onward to the Christian churches.[3]

Was Constantine a lifelong pagan or was he a Christian and for how long?

What, then, is to be made of the various strands of evidence regarding Constantine's status as a Christian? A full answer to this question probably needs to account for two things: first, the fact that Christianity was a small minority in the Roman Empire at the time that Constantine rose to power; and second, that Constantine was a politician ruling in a very difficult, even dangerous, environment.

There are no hard statistics, but various estimates place Christians in the Roman Empire at somewhere between 5 and 15 percent of the total population and suggest that they were more heavily concentrated in the eastern half of the empire than in the west. In the east, their numbers might have been as high as 20 percent of the population.[4] These percentages correspond to between 5 and 7.5 million Christians across the empire—a very significant number of people, but definitely a minority.

Under Constantine's patronage, Christian numbers increased dramatically, but not overwhelmingly so. The final Christianization of the empire was still not accomplished even in the time of his son, Constantine II. Between A.D. 361 and 363, Constantine's nephew, Julian the Apostate, even tried to repaganize the empire. He was unsuccessful, however, and after Julian's time, Christianity became increasingly dominant in the Roman Empire. All of this, though, was future when Constantine took power. He governed a people who were largely non-Christian. Indeed, during Constantine's years in Diocletian's court, being a Christian became increasingly difficult. In fact, it could be a death sentence.

Here is where a concept suggested by T. G. Elliott might be helpful. He speaks of "army Christianity," and "the more tolerant Christianity of the [army] camp,"[5] and contrasts this type of Christianity with the Christianity of the martyrs.

During Diocletian's persecution of Christians, for example, Christians, particularly those in leadership positions in the church and society, faced very difficult decisions. Should they comply when the Roman authorities demanded that they hand over their Scriptures? Should they comply when forced to offer sacrifice to a pagan god? Some Christians chose to die rather than do so. Some, believing that martyrs would gain immediate access to heaven, even voluntarily gave themselves up to the authorities, admitting that they were Christians, so they could be tortured and die as martyrs of the faith. Others, though, compromised. Some fled. Some turned over the Christian writings. And some even took part in pagan ceremonies.

After A.D. 312, when Constantine was able to enforce his pro-Christian edicts in Africa, he discovered a divided church there. Christians who had fled or compromised their faith in order to survive during the persecution were despised by those who had stayed and suffered.

What was true of Christians during times of persecution was continuously true of Christians who were in the army, and there were significant numbers of them. Sacrifices and auguries were a regular part of Roman army life, and a Christian soldier would have to be present at such occasions. The legions of the army fought under their own standards, which more rigorous Christians would see as idolatrous. Thus, a Christian in the Roman legions would need to be able to make some sort of accommodation to all of this. Such a Christian has a very different attitude than that of the Christian martyrs. Any Christian would find it almost impossible not to make some accommodations to the regular pagan sacrifices that were part of Roman civic life. At times, this became a matter of personal survival. This was the world in which Constantine lived.

It has been suggested that Constantine's mother may have been a lifelong Christian. Certainly, later in her life when Constantine achieved power, she was an ardent Christian. Constantine's father treated Christians in his territory with leniency, which might indicate that he was an "army Christian,"[6] although it is possible that he might have been influenced by Christians he knew or by Constantine's mother.

Of the roughly 420 laws that have survived and can be attributed to Constantine during his time as Caesar and Augustus, about 30 are unlikely to have been enacted unless Constantine had been a Christian. These are spread throughout his whole time in power and include not only laws restoring property to Christians and Christian churches but even legislation allowing certain issues to be transferred from a court of law to a Christian bishop's court. Other laws deal with tax exemptions for Christian clergy, allowing worship in Christian churches on Sunday, and removing the requirement for a public official to offer sacrifices as part of his duties. This last ruling made it possible for Jews to hold public office, and further legislation limited the percentage of Jews that could take advantage of this provision.[7]

The overall result of these laws, although they gave advantages to Christianity, did not force Christianity on the peoples in the Roman Empire. Constantine was evenhanded in his dealings with different religious groups. In sum, Constantine was a politician, and a very successful one at that. Under his rule, Christians were still a minority, even though singled out for preferential treatment. At the same time, pagan temples were left unmolested in the western empire, and Constantine did not cast aside his duties as a civic leader, even when they involved priesthoods and temples.

On the other hand, Constantine's own religious preference was relatively visible. Before a crucial battle in A.D. 312, he saw a vision of a cross of light formed in the heavens above the sun, and bearing the inscription "Conquer by this sign." From that time Constantine adopted a Christian symbol incorporating a cross and the Greek letter *rho* (to form the first two letters of the name *Christ*) as his special sign. He put this symbol on a standard for his army and prayed a prayer acceptable to the Christians' God before that and subsequent battles. Furthermore, Christian church leaders became part of his entourage from that time onward. His pagan soldiers, polytheists by and large, would no doubt have seen Constantine's devotion to his particular God as an example of the piety of one of their leaders, many of whom, while believing in more than one god, often had a special relationship with one deity.[8]

23

In Constantine, political expediency often intersected with religious conviction, yet it is hard to consider his words and actions and not conclude that he was a Christian. But why, then, was Constantine not baptized until just before he died? Such a practice was not unknown among Christians at the time. It came about like this. Believers agreed that baptism washed away one's sins. *But what about sin after baptism?* Christians were not agreed on how many times a believer could sin after baptism and still be saved. Some felt that even one sin would be too many. A Christian prophet at Rome, the so-called Shepherd of Hermas, claimed to have had a vision assuring him that Christians could sin once after baptism and still be saved. But only once![9] Thus, many Christians concluded that the right time to be baptized was just before death—that way there simply would be no time to sin following baptism! It is impossible to know how much the frequent necessity for waging war and the occasional assassination that marked Constantine's career influenced him in delaying his baptism. But in any event, his decision to be baptized late in life was not entirely exceptional among Christians of the time.

Constantine will reappear in several of the later chapters in this book, but even now it is possible to comment on one aspect of the conspiracy theory advanced by Teabing. Was Constantine "a lifelong pagan who was baptized on his deathbed, too weak to protest"?[10] It is rather difficult to conceive of Constantine as being too weak to protest even on his deathbed. Furthermore, while it is possible to see in some of his actions a secret sympathy with paganism, it is much more likely that these particular actions resulted from political expediency. Constantine, let it be said, was a very able politician at a time when politics was played with life-and-death seriousness, literally. Thus many of his actions were either consciously or unconsciously ambiguous—both Christians and pagans could applaud what he did. Such was politically wise when working in an environment where Christians were but a minority of the population. So, it appears unlikely that Constantine was a lifelong pagan. Let's add this conclusion to the chart showing the various elements of the conspiracy theory put forward by the character Teabing in *The Da Vinci Code:*

Constantine's "conspiracy" as alleged by the characters in *The Da Vinci Code*	
Claim by the "Royal Historian," Teabing:	True or False?
"Constantine . . . was a lifelong pagan who was baptized on his deathbed, too weak to protest" (p. 313).	**Unlikely**
"By fusing pagan symbols, dates, and rituals into the growing Christian tradition, he created a kind of hybrid religion that was acceptable to both parties" (p. 314).	
"Christianity honored the Jewish Sabbath of Saturday, but Constantine shifted it to coincide with the pagan's veneration day of the sun" (pp. 314, 315).	
"Until that moment in history [the Council of Nicaea], Jesus was viewed by His followers as a mortal prophet . . . a great and powerful man, but a man nonetheless. A mortal" (p. 315).	
"To rewrite the history books, Constantine knew he would need a bold stroke. From this sprang the most profound moment in Christian history. . . . Constantine commissioned and financed a new Bible, which omitted those gospels which spoke of Christ's human traits and embellished those gospels that made Him godlike" (pp. 316, 317).	
"Mary Magdalene was the Holy Vessel. She was the chalice that bore the royal bloodline of Jesus Christ. She was the womb that bore the lineage" (p. 336).	

So much, then, for whether or not Constantine was a Christian. What about the claims that he actively chose which documents should be in the New Testament and that he suppressed many early Christian documents that did not fit the type of Christianity that he wanted to create? In answering this question, we will find that murder, mystery, and mayhem occur in real life as well as in fiction; all of these elements surround the discovery of some of the gospels that were not included in the New Testament. These are the gospels that were found in Nag Hammadi in Egypt.

CHAPTER 3

Real Life Murder, Mystery, and Mayhem: The Nag Hammadi Gospels

The Nag Hammadi gospels were discovered in the midst of a series of bloody murders undertaken in search of revenge. On the night of May 7, 1945, an Egyptian night watchman killed a marauder. By midmorning the next day, he was murdered, in turn, as an act of blood vengeance. His widow told her seven sons to keep their mattocks sharp—that is, to be ready to defend themselves and to avenge their father's death. This was the situation in December of that year when two of the night watchman's sons—Muhammad and Khalifah 'Ali—discovered a jar buried near a rock where they had been digging for fertilizer.

At first, Muhammad was reluctant to open the jar, thinking it might contain a jinn or evil spirit. But on reflection, he thought it equally possible that the jar might contain gold, so he broke it open with his mattock. Within were a number of ancient books written on papyrus and bound in leather. During the early Christian period, written materials, especially those relating to Christianity, tended to be published in codex (or book form), rather than in scrolls. The books the brothers found were later determined to contain fifty-two small writings, called tractates. These tractates had been copied onto papyrus scrolls, which had then been stitched into book form and given covers made of leather reinforced with further papyrus sheets glued together. But this is getting ahead in the story somewhat.

Apparently a total of seven camel drivers were also present when the manuscripts were discovered, and Muhammad divided the books into seven equal piles. There were not enough for each driver to get two books each, so Muhammad tore one or more of the books apart in order to make equal piles. It turned out that he need not have done so, as the camel drivers declined to take any of the newly discovered materials. So Muhammad gathered up the writings into a single pile, wrapped the books in his white headdress, and took them back to his house, where he dumped them on the straw his mother had gathered to fuel her cooking fire. Some of the covers and pages ended up in the fire![1]

About a month after the discovery, not far from Muhammad 'Ali's house, a peasant, named Ahmad, fell asleep next to a jar of sugar cane molasses that he had for sale. A neighbor pointed him out to Muhammad as the murderer of his father. The brothers gathered and attacked Ahmad with their mattocks; they killed him, ripped out his heart, and devoured it—a horrific act of blood revenge.

Ahmad was the son of the local sheriff, who was so unpopular that no one could be found to testify about the murder of his son. However, Muhammad was fearful that police would search his house in connection with Ahmad's murder and find the books he had discovered. So he entrusted them to the local Coptic (Christian) priest—probably because the books were written in Coptic, a dialect of Egyptian written using Greek letters. The priest's brother-in-law saw the books, recognized their potential value, and suggested that he try to find out what they might be worth. Eventually, a sum of £300 changed hands, £50 of which accompanied one of the books to the Coptic Museum in Cairo, where it was deposited on October 4, 1946. The rest of the books were scattered. Eventually, however, most of the thirteen books ended up in the Cairo Coptic Museum. Then slowly, as scholars were able to do their work, the different tractates were published, beginning with

The Gospel of Thomas in 1959. Their publication in 1977 as *The Nag Hammadi Library in English* (James M. Robinson, editor) has made the books widely available to those who are not specialists in Coptic studies. This is the true life background of murder and mystery that lies behind the Nag Hammadi gospels.

The Gospel of Thomas

Several of the Nag Hammadi tractates are identified as gospels. These gospels include *The Gospel of Truth*, *The Gospel of Thomas*, *The Gospel of Philip*, and *The Gospel of the Egyptians*. To these might also be added two further gospels: *The Gospel of Mary*, which because of its similar themes, Robinson included in *The Nag Hammadi Library in English* even though it did not belong with the Nag Hammadi discoveries, and, more recently published, *The Gospel of Judas*. This group of gospels is quite different in nature from the four Gospels included in the Bible—Matthew, Mark, Luke, and John. We will be looking at those differences in the next few chapters of this book.

Of the Nag Hammadi gospels that have survived that are *not* found in the Bible, *The Gospel of Thomas* has attracted the most attention from scholars, and quite correctly so. *The Gospel of Thomas* has the potential to include authentic sayings of Jesus that are otherwise lost. It also preserves very old versions of many of the sayings of Jesus that are already known from the four Gospels found in the Bible.

The Gospel of Thomas begins with the following words:

These are the secret sayings which the living Jesus spoke and which Didymus Judas Thomas wrote down. (1) And he said, "Whoever finds the interpretation of these sayings will not experience death." (2) Jesus said, "Let him who seeks continue seeking until he finds. When he finds, he will become troubled. When he becomes troubled, he will be astonish, and he will rule over the All. . . . [2]

In fact, *The Gospel of Thomas* is a collection of sayings attributed to Jesus. Some of them are sayings that are found in the biblical Gospels. For example, *The Gospel of Thomas* 9 reads:

> Jesus said, "Now the sower went out, took a handful (of seeds), and scattered them. Some fell on the road; the birds came and gathered them up. Others fell on rock, did not take root in the soil, and did not produce ears. And others fell on thorns; they choked the seed(s) and worms ate them. And others fell on the good soil and produced good fruit: it bore sixty per measure and a hundred and twenty per measure."

If we compare this to the parable of the sower found in Matthew 13:1–9, 18–23; Mark 4:1–9, 13–20; and Luke 8:4–8, 11–15, we will see that *The Gospel of Thomas* 9 is telling the same parable but in different words. Furthermore, *The Gospel of Thomas* is missing the interpretation of the parable found in the biblical Gospels. These features suggest that *The Gospel of Thomas* might actually contain a version of this parable that was preserved independently of the traditions that found their way into Matthew, Mark, and Luke.

There is considerable debate as to how much credibility to give to the sayings of Jesus found in *The Gospel of Thomas*. Some writers give great credence to *The Gospel of Thomas* as a source.[3] I do not. The last saying of the gospel (*The Gospel of Thomas* 114) illustrates the problems that I have with the gospel as a whole:

> (114) Simon Peter said to them, "Let Mary leave us, for women are not worthy of Life." Jesus said, "I myself shall lead her in order to make her male, so that she too may become a living spirit resembling you males. For every woman who will make herself male will enter the Kingdom of Heaven."

Call me cynical, but I don't think Jesus actually said those words! It doesn't fit what else I know about Him from the biblical Gospels. I concede that *The Gospel of Thomas* is independent of the biblical Gospels. Thus it could provide another version of authentic words of Jesus known already from the biblical Gospels, and it could also contain authentic sayings of Jesus that are otherwise lost to us. But my problem is that I do not know which of these sayings can actually be traced back to Jesus. *The Gospel of Thomas*—at least as we know it—is from a much later time period than the biblical Gospels[4] and is influenced strongly by ideas that could loosely be described as Gnostic.[5] What the term *Gnostic* means is perhaps best explained by looking in closer detail at *The Gospel of Judas.* And we will do just that in the next chapter.

CHAPTER 4 | The Gospel of Judas

The few vague details that are known about how *The Gospel of Judas* came into the hands of the Maecenas Foundation for Ancient Art in the year 2000 hint of a fascinating story—no murder this time, but certainly mystery and perhaps a touch of skulduggery.

The Gospel of Judas was part of an ancient codex (or book) that first became visible to the academic world in 1983 in Geneva, when three experts were given the opportunity to briefly examine a manuscript that was for sale. Impressed by the importance of such ancient manuscript discoveries as the Dead Sea Scrolls and the Nag Hammadi library, the seller was seeking at least three million dollars for the manuscript, a price ten times what the three experts could possibly raise, so no sale occurred at the time. The manuscript was subsequently taken to the United States. But a buyer could not be found in the United States either, and the ancient document was apparently left in a safety deposit box in a bank at Hicksville, Long Island, New York, for many years.

In 2000 the manuscript was finally purchased by antiquities dealer Frieda Nussberger-Tchacos, who was unable to persuade Yale University to acquire it. The manuscript was briefly in the control of Bruce Ferrini, an opera singer turned dealer in old manuscripts. At some point the pages had been divided in half horizontally so that the top and bottom of each page were not attached to each other, and it is alleged that while the manuscript was in Ferrini's control, the pages of the bottom half of the manuscript were rearranged so that some of the more interesting pages appeared at the top.[1] Furthermore, photographs of the manuscript began to circulate at this time, showing a confusing mix of mismatched top and bottom halves of some pages.[2] Ferrini also nearly destroyed the manuscript by freezing it. He probably intended to slow the rate of decomposition, but instead, the freezing process "produced the partial destruction of the sap holding the fibres of the papyrus together making it significantly more fragile."[3] Eventually, the manuscript ended up in Switzerland, in a deal that involved the Maecenas Foundation, which agreed to turn the document over to the Coptic Museum in Egypt after taking steps to preserve it from further deterioration, and the *National Geographic* magazine, which agreed to publicize and publish the manuscript. Rodolphe Kasser announced this arrangement on July 1, 2004, in Paris, at the Eighth Congress of the International Association for Coptic Studies. The announcement aroused considerable speculation regarding what the newly recovered gospel might contain. The year 2006 has seen the publication of an English translation of *The Gospel of Judas* as it has been reconstructed to date. Despite the deliberate rearrangement of the bottom half of many of the pages and the fact that the manuscript has disintegrated into many pieces, some of which are still unplaced, the translation, edited by Rodolphe Kasser, Marvin Meyer, and Gregor Wurst, enables the reader to gain a relatively good understanding of what *The Gospel of Judas* actually says.

The name *Judas* is the Greek version of the Hebrew name *Judah*. It was a popular name in the time of Jesus as indicated by the fact that no less than two of Jesus' twelve disciples were called Judas ("Judas son of James, and Judas Iscariot, who became a traitor"; see Luke 6:16). In addition, one of Jesus' brothers was also called Judas (see Matthew 13:55). Judas, the brother of Jesus, contributed the book called Jude to the New Testament (see Jude 1). Translators of the New Testament usually call him Jude, presumably to differentiate him from the more infamous Judas Iscariot, although the Greek clearly identifies him as Judas *(Ioudas)* in Jude 1, and many English language Bibles give a note indicating the name is actually Judas, not Jude.

There is no doubt as to which of these three men named Judas the newly rediscovered gospel refers to. *The Gospel of Judas* clearly claims to be "The secret account of the revelation that Jesus spoke in conversation with Judas Iscariot during a week three days before he celebrated Passover" (p. 19).[4]

The Gospel of Judas is quite brief and consists of a series of dialogues, sometimes between Jesus and the twelve disciples, but often just between Jesus and Judas. Early in the gospel, Judas shows himself superior to the other disciples, whereupon Jesus says to him, "Step away from the others and I shall tell you the mysteries of the Kingdom" (p. 23). In a later dialogue, the disciples are troubled by a vision they have seen of twelve priests sacrificing at an altar. Jesus tells them, "The cattle you have seen brought for sacrifice are the people you lead astray" (p. 27). These are but two places in *The Gospel of Judas* that imply, or state, that only Judas, of all Jesus' disciples, understands the true nature of the kingdom of God and the other teachings of Jesus. According to *The Gospel of Judas,* the rest of the disciples are leading people astray.

A significant part of the gospel is devoted to a dialogue in which Jesus talks to Judas about "a great and boundless realm, whose extent no generation of angels has seen" (p. 33). The gospel says, "And a luminous cloud appeared there. He [Jesus] said, 'Let an angel come into being as my attendant.' A great angel, the enlightened divine Self-Generated, emerged from the cloud" (p. 34). This great angel caused four other angels to come into being, and very shortly "myriads without number [of angels] came into being" (p. 34). Next "He [the great angel] made seventy-two luminaries appear in the incorruptible generation" (p. 36). The text then explains, "The twelve aeons of the twelve luminaries constitute their father, with six heavens for each aeon, so that there are seventy-two heavens for the seventy-two luminaries." (p. 36). Finally, we come to an angel named Nebro and Yaldabaoth: "And look, from the cloud there appeared an [angel] whose face flashed with fire and whose appearance was defiled with blood. His name was Nebro, which means 'rebel'; others call him Yaldabaoth. Another angel, Saklas, also come from the cloud" (pp. 37, 38). According to *The Gospel of Judas* Saklas "said to his angels, 'Let us create a human being after the likeness and after the image' " (p. 39).

This great interest in the aeons and the different heavens, together with the idea that the creator of the Old Testament was an inferior divine being who made a mistake in creating the world, links *The Gospel of Judas* with other writings described as Gnostic writings, from the Greek word *gnōsis*, meaning "knowledge." The early church father Irenaeus said this type of writing represented "knowledge *(gnōsis)*, falsely so called." There was a whole movement—Gnosticism—in the early Christian church based on the idea that only those who managed to attain a certain level of special knowledge would be saved. We will look at Gnostics and Gnosticism in the next chapter. For the moment it is probably enough to point out that the three angelic names in *The Gospel of Judas*—Nebro, Yaldabaoth, and Saklas—all have meanings. *The Gospel of Judas* itself explains that *Nebro* means "rebel." *Saklas* means "fool" in Aramaic. The name *Yaldabaoth*, which is used in other Gnostic writings to refer to the creator God of the Old Testament, probably means "child of chaos" in Aramaic.

Some of the gaps still remaining in the manuscript, as we have it, occur at places that obscure what looks like an important part of the explanation of why Judas would betray Jesus. After nine missing lines that follow a comment on baptism, and three more missing lines following something about sacrifices to Saklas, Jesus says, "But you will exceed all of them. For you will sacrifice the man that clothes me." Bart D. Ehrman sees this comment as the key to understanding the perspective of the gospel.

Earlier in *The Gospel of Judas,* Judas had asked, "[Rabb]i, what kind of fruit does this generation produce?" and Jesus had replied, "The souls of every human generation will die. When these people, however, have completed the time of the kingdom and the spirit leaves them, their bodies will die but their souls will be alive, and they will be taken up" (p. 30). Thus, according to *The Gospel of Judas,* the ideal spiritual outcome is for the immortal soul to be "taken up." It is not stated, but presumably the ideal is that the soul be "taken up" into the ranks of the "incorruptible generation." So what does it mean when Jesus says to Judas, "You will sacrifice the man that clothes me"? According to Bart Ehrman, the "delivering up" of Jesus by Judas to the Jewish religious authorities was in fact a "faithful act of his [Jesus'] most intimate companion and faithful follower, the one who handed him over to his death that he might return to his heavenly home."[5]

This interpretation of *The Gospel of Judas* explains why the gospel finishes with these words: "They [the high priests] approached Judas and said to him, 'What are you doing here? You are Jesus' disciples.' Judas answered them as they wished. And he received some money and handed him over to them. The Gospel of Judas" (p. 45). From the perspective of the Gospels found in the Christian Bible, the "handing over" of Jesus by Judas is an odd place to end the story. But it is indeed the way *The Gospel of Judas* ends. The final words, "The Gospel of Judas," are the title given to the gospel. Indeed, from the perspective of *The Gospel of Judas,* the death of Jesus releases His soul to return to its place amongst the incorruptibles.

One can immediately see that this is a very different understanding of Christianity than that found in the Bible. Jesus' death is seen as freeing His spirit from His body, but it is not given any importance in the salvation of His followers. Instead, for *The Gospel of Judas,* it is the teachings of Jesus that are important, not the Cross. But Jesus' teachings as portrayed in *The Gospel of Judas* are very different from His teachings as found in Matthew, Mark, Luke, and John. In *The Gospel of Judas,* Jesus is concerned with philosophical speculation on heavenly beings, giving secret information about the 12 aeons, the 72 heavens, the 360 firmaments, and the 72 luminaries and their relationship to the self-generated angel. This is the knowledge that Jesus gives to Judas. The type of Christianity represented by the rest of the disciples is wrong, at least according to *The Gospel of Judas*.

A mirror image of this thinking can also be found among those early Christians who did follow the teachings of the rest of the apostles. Irenaeus, Bishop of Lyon in Gaul (a Roman province roughly corresponding with modern France), went so far as to link *The Gospel of Judas* with a group that he labels Cainites. Irenaeus makes no bones about it—Cainites are wrong; they are "heretics." Modern scholarship has usually applied the label *Gnosticism* to many of the "heresies" identified by Irenaeus. It is worth looking at Gnosticism a little more closely because it can provide a background against which one can evaluate these "gospels," such as *The Gospel of Judas,* that did not make it into the New Testament.

CHAPTER 5 | Gnosticism

For many years, the only evidence that could be used to form a picture of Gnosticism was what its enemies said about it, particularly a work written about A.D. 185 by the church father Irenaeus, called *Refutation and Overthrow of Knowledge Falsely So-Called,* or more usually, *Against Heresies.*[1]

The contribution of Irenaeus

Irenaeus begins his work by stating that he intends "to the best of my ability, with brevity and clearness to set forth the opinions of those who are now promulgating heresy."[2] Modern readers find his description neither very brief nor very clear. He launches into a general description of the position of the heretics, beginning with a description of the pre-existent *Aeon,* and a more detailed outline of the names and positions of all the heavenly beings than we find in *The Gospel of Judas.* There is little point in following the confusing procession of *Nous* (mind), *Monogenes* (only-begotten), *Aletheia* (truth), *Logos* (word), *Zoe* (life), *Anthropos* (man), *Ecclesia* (church), etc., which are arranged three ways—an Ogdoad (set of eight), a Decad (set of ten), and a Duodecad (set of twelve), together making up the thirty Aeons of the *Pleroma* (book 1, chapter I).

Having listed the thirty *Aeons,* Irenaeus traces the formation of the Christ (chapter II) and also the emergence of the *Demiurge,* also known as *Metropator* (coming only from a mother, without a father) and *Apator* (literally, "without a father"). This being created all material substances by forming them from the three passions of fear, grief, and perplexity (chapters IV and V). The underlying idea is that material substances are inferior to the spiritual realm.

Humans, apparently, come in three kinds—material, animal, or spiritual. At death, the material go into corruption. The spiritual, on the other hand, are released from their bodies and will rejoin the other incorruptible spiritual beings in the *Pleroma.* The fate of the animal depend on decisions made during life (chapter VII).

After giving a general summary of the position of the heretics, Irenaeus goes on to survey the ideas of individual groups, highlighting the connections between them. Of particular interest is his mention of *The Gospel of Judas* toward the end of this recitation. He names one of the groups, Cainites, which he describes in the following words:

> Others again declare that Cain derived his being from the Power above, and acknowledge that Esau, Korah, the Sodomites, and all such persons, are related to themselves. . . . They declare that Judas the traitor was thoroughly acquainted with these things, and that he alone, knowing the truth as no others did, accomplished the mystery of the betrayal. . . . They produce a fictitious history of this kind, which they style the Gospel of Judas" (book 1, chapter XXXI).

Irenaeus, then, links *The Gospel of Judas* with one of a wide spectrum of groups promulgating ideas he defines as heresy. He even uses the adjective *gnostic* to describe some of these groups and individuals, but the term *Gnosticism* was not coined until the year 1669.[3]

In the modern era, the various Gnostic groups have fascinated biblical scholars and church historians, even before the discoveries of documents actually coming from these groups. Scholars asked, for example, if Gnosticism lay behind some of the problems Paul faced with the believers at Corinth since the troublemakers at Corinth talk a lot about knowledge (*gnōsis*)—see 1 Corinthians 1:22; 2:1, 5–8; 3:18, 19; 8:1. In other letters of Paul, various troublemakers in the church speak of myths and endless genealogies (1 Timothy 1:4; compare to Titus 3:9), and in Galatians Paul warns his readers not to become enslaved again to the elemental spirits by observing special days and months and seasons and years (see Galatians 4:9, 10). There is a perennial discussion among biblical scholars as to whether some form of Gnostic ideas have influenced Paul's opponents and therefore lie behind these comments of Paul.

Church historians have also been fascinated by Gnosticism and the place it has in the spectrum of early Christian groups. Some speculative Gnostic ideas were apparently influenced strongly by Greek philosophy. At the other end of the spectrum were groups of Christians that still clung to aspects of Judaism.

The contribution of the ancient Gnostic documents

The discovery of the Nag Hammadi documents, as well as such manuscripts as *The Gospel of Mary* and other documents produced by the Gnostics themselves, has enabled scholars to examine the actual writings of these various groups of early Christians. The differences between these documents are interesting. Scholars have divided the writings into at least three separate groups, based on their content: Valentinianism, Sethianism, and Hermeticism.

Valentinianism traces its roots back to an important second-century Christian poet and theologian, Valentinus. Several different writings can be attributed to this group, including a very heavy philosophical work called *The Gospel of Truth*. Sethianism derives its name from the Sethians, one of the groups Irenaeus mentions in his work *Against Heresies*. *The Gospel of Judas* is classified as Sethian. Hermeticism was known before the discovery of the Nag Hammadi documents, and since several of the newly discovered documents show similar ideas, they have been classified as Hermetic. The following table lists some of the differences between two of these groups:[4]

Differences between Valentinianism and Sethianism		
	Valentinianism	Sethianism
Who is the Savior?	Jesus is the primary Savior.	There are a number of possible saviors, including many female figures.
Creator of this world	Viewed partially positively	Viewed negatively
Situation of humanity	Ignorance and error	A battle against forces of worldly desire and passion
Salvation	Suffering and death are illusions to be overcome by knowledge.	Ascetic self-rule offers protection against demonic forces.
Place of history and myth	Myth a timeless portrayal of the soul's situation in the world	Salvation is found in history, starting with Adam and Eve.
Number of types of humans	Three (includes less spiritually advanced "psychics")	Two—the saved and the unsaved

Obviously, there are some large differences in belief between the various Gnostic groups. Therefore, some scholars question whether it is appropriate to use a single term, *Gnosticism,* to describe them all.[5] Karen King, for example, criticizes the use of the term on exactly these grounds. She says it belongs to the disputes of some of the early apologists of Christianity, such as Irenaeus. It is part of "us" versus "them" language, like the dichotomy between Christian and pagan, or Christian and Jew. The word *pagan* covers an enormously wide range of belief and practice. Essentially, the word means "somebody who is not a Christian." In fact, it is rather like the words *Gentile* and *Greek* as they are used in the New Testament (see Acts 21:25; Romans 10:12; Galatians 3:28; Colossians 3:11, etc.). The term *Gentile* just means "non-Jew."

But is the fact that a term covers a wide variety of phenomena a good enough reason to abandon it? I don't think so. Consider some other terms in common use. The term *Christian,* for example, covers people of very diverse beliefs and practices. It describes Dominican monks, Southern Baptists, Anglicans, Pentecostals, and a whole host of different groups. Likewise, *Islam* is a term that describes a very diverse set of beliefs and practices, at least from the perspective of the Sunni and Shi'a! Nor have we abandoned terms such as *middle class* and *working class,* despite the very wide range of groups these words describe. Such general categories serve as useful terms that describe a certain group of people or grouping of ideas that share enough common characteristics to make a generalized description worth using. The terms remain because of their usefulness.

Likewise, *Gnosticism* is a useful term for describing a variety of different groups, claiming to be authentic Christians, but whose understanding of Christianity placed such a great emphasis on philosophy that little room was left for the cross of Jesus or His teachings as they are found in the New Testament. The Christianity of the Gnostics concerned itself with speculations about the heavenly aeons and claimed salvation came through secret knowledge rather than through the death of Jesus on the cross. Gnosticism lacked interest in the doings of the historical Jesus and did not speak about the resurrection of the body. Most likely they would have been offended by the idea of a physical resurrection, like some of those living in Corinth at an earlier time who claimed "there is no resurrection of the dead" (1 Corinthians 15:12). The Gnostics were antagonistic to the segment of Christianity represented by those who accepted the New Testament and who found themselves in churches managed by clergy. The Gnostics were certainly made up of diverse groups of people, but they had enough ideas in common that the term *Gnosticism* is useful to describe a particular broad stream of Christianity. The term is too useful to set aside.[6] Even so, we should probably talk of *Gnosticisms,* rather than of *Gnosticism.*

All this provides a necessary background to *The Gospel of Mary* and *The Gospel of Philip*, the two non–New Testament gospels that the character Teabing quotes so extensively in *The Da Vinci Code* as he explains to Sophie about the relationship between Mary Magdalene and Jesus.

CHAPTER 6 | Mary Magdalene and the Gospels of Mary and Philip

Our investigations, which started as a response to a conversation in the outskirts of Paris between Sophie, Langdon, and Teabing, have led us to ancient Rome, Nag Hammadi, and a modern town in Egypt, as well as to Zurich and New York. Some of the adventures described have been as dangerous and mysterious as anything found in *The Da Vinci Code*. But let's return now to the conversation found in *The Da Vinci Code*, chapter 58, in which Teabing finally leads Sophie to a full understanding of who he thinks is the Holy Grail.

Teabing on The Gospel of Philip

Sophie, now convinced that the individual sitting next to Jesus in Leonardo da Vinci's painting of the Last Supper is a woman, naturally wants to know who she is. Teabing replies that she is none other than Mary Magdalene.

"The prostitute?" Sophie asks with some surprise.

No, says Teabing. "That unfortunate misconception is the legacy of a smear campaign launched by the early Church." Teabing further explains that in its efforts to convince the world that the prophet Jesus was divine, the church omitted any "gospels that described *earthy* aspects of Jesus' life. . . . More specifically, her marriage to Jesus Christ."[1]

In support of this startling claim, Teabing brings out a large book, titled *The Gnostic Gospels*. He explains that they are "photocopies of the Nag Hammadi and Dead Sea Scrolls. . . . The earliest Christian records." He reads a section from *The Gospel of Philip*. The translation cited in *The Da Vinci Code* is essentially the one found in *The Nag Hammadi Library*, edited by James M. Robinson. It is the same translation of the Nag Hammadi documents that I have used in this book. There is one big difference, however. The text in *The Da Vinci Code* lacks the square brackets the translators have used to indicate where they have had to supply a word because something is missing in the original document. As you can see from the number of words in square brackets, the Nag Hammadi text for the following passage from *The Gospel of Philip* (quoted in *The Da Vinci Code*) is rather damaged. Remember, the words in brackets are missing from the original document and have been supplied by the translators using their best "guess" of what the original may have said:

> And the companion of the [Saviour is] Mary Magdalene. [Christ loved] her more than [all] the disciples [and used to] kiss her [often] on her [mouth]. The rest of [the disciples were offended] by it [and expressed disapproval.] They said to him, "Why do you love her more than all of us?"[2]

In *The Da Vinci Code*, this quotation is immediately followed by an exchange between Sophie and Teabing:

> The words surprised Sophie, and yet they hardly seemed conclusive. "It says nothing of marriage."
>
> "*Au contraire.*" Teabing smiled, pointing to the first line. "As any Aramaic scholar will tell you, the word *companion,* in those days, literally meant *spouse.*"[3]

The Gospel of Philip: Was Jesus married?

Several points about this crucial exchange between Teabing and Sophie demand comment. In a later chapter, we will look at the importance of Teabing's untrue claim that the Nag Hammadi and Dead Sea Scrolls are the earliest Christian records. They are not! In fact, although the Dead Sea Scrolls may predate the Gospels found in the New Testament, they are definitely *not* Christian. The Nag Hammadi documents, on the other hand, are Christian writings, but they were produced much later than any document found in the New Testament. But more on the significance of this later.

Second, while the passage Teabing cites from *The Gospel of Philip* is certainly one of the more sensational passages in the Nag Hammadi library, it is actually a reconstruction of a very fragmentary text. Here is how the actual text reads if we leave out the words that are missing from the original document and which the translators have added. I've included a previous sentence to provide some context:

> As for the Wisdom who is called "the barren," she is the mother . . . angels. And the companion of the . . . Mary Magdalene . . . her more than . . . disciples . . . kiss her . . . on her . . . the rest of . . . by it . . . They said to him, "Why do you love her more than all of us?"[4]

Given that framework of words, is it possible to accurately fill in those that are missing? Where, for example, did Jesus often kiss Mary? On the cheek? On her forehead? Yes, the missing word probably is *mouth,* as the translators suggest, and the rest of their reconstruction, quoted above, is probably not that far from the original.

But Teabing's statement that the word *companion* literally means "spouse" is very much open to dispute. So also is his suggestion that the word is an Aramaic word. Although Jesus probably spoke Aramaic, *The Gospel of Philip* was originally written in Greek and then translated into Coptic. The particular word translated "companion" has nothing to do with Aramaic. It is a loan word from Greek and elsewhere means "companion," nothing more.[5] It is not impossible that the passage in *The Gospel of Philip* intends the word to mean "sexual partner" or even "spouse," but this would be an unusual use of the word. Besides, we hear of Jesus' mother, brothers, and sisters, in the canonical Gospels (see Matthew 13:55). Would we not also expect to hear if He had a wife?[6] In fact, outside of this rather dubious assertion advanced by Teabing, there is *no* suggestion in the ancient documents that Mary Magdalene was married to Jesus. This point is important enough to warrant quoting Bart Ehrman, a specialist in early Christian literature, especially literature outside of the New Testament. Teabing says, "I shan't bore you with the countless references to Jesus and Magdalene's union," (*The Da Vinci Code,* page 333). However, Bart Ehrman declares

> In *none* of our early Christian sources is there any reference to Jesus' marriage or to his wife. This is true not only of the canonical Gospels of Matthew, Mark, Luke, and John but of all our other Gospels and all of our other early Christians writings put together. There is no allusion to Jesus as married in the writings of Paul, the Gospel of Peter, the Gospel of Philip, the Gospel of Mary, the Gospel of the Nazarenes—and on and on. List every ancient source we have for the historical Jesus, and in none of them is there mention of Jesus being married.[7]

It's true that most Jewish men were married. Elsewhere in the Roman Empire, celibacy surfaces from time to time as a very desirable state. For example, some considered that the very existence of Rome depended on the continued celibate status of the vestal virgins, and horrific penalties were meted out for any vestal virgin straying from this ideal. Emperor Augustus (30 B.C.–A.D. 14) actually introduced legislation requiring adult Roman men to marry; this law was not repealed until the reign of Constantine more than three hundred years later. Yet it is also true that some philosophical and religious circles in the ancient world praised celibacy as an ideal. Celibacy was espoused by some Christians quite early in the history of the church, eventually resulting in the idea of a celibate priesthood. But it was rare to find celibacy promoted as an ideal in Jewish religious circles, although one exception might be the community at Qumran which produced the documents that later became the Dead Sea Scrolls.[8] Some of the Old Testament prophets were single because they were widowed (see Ezekiel 24:15–18). The New Testament does not say whether John the Baptist was married, but the details that are given— he lived in the Judean desert, was clothed in camel-hair garments, and ate locusts and wild honey—tend to give the impression that he was not accompanied by a wife! That Jesus also was single fits His role as a prophet.[9]

Personally, I would not have a problem if it could be proved that Jesus had been married. After all, both the Old and New Testaments consider marriage, and sex within marriage, to be God-ordained and approved. But the evidence that Jesus was married simply is not there.

What, though, does the New Testament have to say about Mary Magdalene?

Mary Magdalene in the New Testament

As a matter of fact, despite the significant role that Mary Magdalene has been given in modern treatments of Jesus (for example, in the rock musical *Jesus Christ Superstar*), she is actually a very minor character in the New Testament Gospels. The name *Mary* occurs in forty-nine different verses, but twenty-one of them are referring to Mary, the mother of Jesus, and a further eleven come from John chapters 11 and 12, which describe the two sisters, Mary and Martha, and how Jesus raised their brother Lazarus from the dead. Some have identified this Mary with Mary Magdalene, but that is not certain by any means.

Mary must have been a popular name in first-century Palestine. Not only do we meet Mary, the mother of Jesus, in the New Testament, we also hear of Mary, the mother of James and Joses (Matthew 27:56; Mark 15:47; Luke 24:10, etc), Mary the wife of Cleophas (John 19:25), and Mary the mother of John Mark (Acts 12:12), as well as an otherwise unidentified Mary known to Paul and living at Rome (Romans 16:6). The "Magdalene" part of the name *Mary Magdalene* distinguishes her from the other Marys in the New Testament and is most likely a reference to the fact that Mary Magdalene comes from the town of Magdala.[10] Mary, the sister of Martha and Lazarus, lived in Bethany. It is not impossible that this is the same woman as Mary Magdalene; after all, people do move from the town of their birth, but no probability can be attached to the suggestion.

Mary Magdalene does play one important role in the New Testament, though. She is among the women who see where Jesus is buried, and she is the one who first meets Jesus after He has risen from the dead (see Matthew 27:56–61; 28:1; Mark 15:40–47; Luke 24:10; John 20:1–18). Aside from this, Mary Magdalene is but one of several women in Jesus' entourage (see Luke 8:1–3). *The Da Vinci Code* perhaps makes too much of the fact, but it is true that the relationships between Jesus and various women were much more relaxed than might have been expected according to the social customs of the day. In allowing Mary the sister of Martha and Lazarus to sit with His disciples while Martha prepared the meal (see Luke 10:39–42), Jesus admitted her into the inner circle of disciples and allowed her to take instruction. This would have been very untypical of the times in which Jesus lived. This is but one incident of several recorded in the Gospels in which Jesus shows an acceptance of women unusual for His day.[11] But does any of this imply that Jesus was actually married to Mary Magdalene? Hardly.

Teabing on The Gospel of Mary

So much, then, for *The Gospel of Philip*. In talking about Mary Magdalene, Teabing also refers to another gospel, *The Gospel of Mary*. The quotation in *The Da Vinci Code* shortens the original somewhat, although it does not change its meaning. Here is the full quotation (this time, the square brackets indicate sections omitted from the quotation as given in *The Da Vinci Code*):

[Andrew answered and said to the brethren, "Say what you (wish to) say about what she has said. I at least do not believe that the Savior said this. For certainly these teachings are strange ideas."] Peter answered [and spoke concerning the same things. He questioned them about the Savior:] "Did he really speak privately with a woman (and) not openly to us? Are we to turn about and all listen to her? Did he prefer her to us?"

[Then Mary wept and said to Peter, "My brother Peter, what do you think? Do you think that I thought this up myself in my heart, or that I am lying about the Savior?"] Levi answered and said to Peter, "Peter, you have always been hot-tempered. Now I see you contending against the women like the adversaries. But if the Savior made her worthy, who are you indeed to reject her? Surely the Savior knows her very well. That is why he loved her more than us."[12]

Teabing makes much of these words. He says to Sophie:

"According to these unaltered gospels, it was not *Peter* to whom Christ gave directions with which to establish the Christian Church. It was *Mary Magdalene*."

Sophie looked at him. "You're saying the Christian Church was to be carried on by a *woman?*"

"That was the plan. Jesus was the original feminist. He intended for the future of His Church to be in the hands of Mary Magdalene."

"And Peter had a problem with that," Langdon said.[13]

The Gospel of Mary

In saying this, Teabing and Langdon actually report fairly accurately the claim made by *The Gospel of Mary,* or at least those parts of it that have survived (the first six pages are missing). What is left of *The Gospel of Mary* begins with the tail end of a conversation between Jesus and Peter, in which, among other things, Jesus answers Peter's question, "What is the sin of the world," with the answer, "There is no sin, but it is you that make sin . . ." Soon, thereafter, Jesus leaves. Mary greets the disciples and turns "their hearts to the Good, and they began to discuss the words of the [Savior]."

> Peter said to Mary, "Sister, we know that the Savior loved you more than the rest of women. Tell us the words of the Savior which you remember—which you know (but) we do not nor have we heard them." Mary answered and said, "What is hidden from you I will proclaim to you."[14]

Thus, Peter is portrayed as acknowledging that Mary had a special relationship with Jesus. So he asks her what Jesus had told her that He didn't tell the other disciples. Mary obliges, but unfortunately much of her speech is missing, although one can see that it begins in a manner not unlike it ends—with ideas similar to other Gnostic gospels, such as *The Gospel of Truth.* The following is a sample taken from toward the end of Mary's speech:

> When the soul had overcome the third power, it went upwards and saw the fourth power, (which) took seven forms. The

first form is darkness, the second desire, the third ignorance, the fourth is the excitement of death, the fifth is the kingdom of the flesh, the sixth is the foolish wisdom of flesh, the seventh is the wrathful wisdom. These are the seven [powers] of wrath. They ask the soul, "Whence do you come, slayer of men, or where are you going, conqueror of space?"[15]

It is not surprising, therefore, when Andrew responds, "Say what you (wish to) say about what she has said. I at least do not believe that the Savior said this. For certainly these teachings are strange ideas." Peter also refuses to believe that these words come from Jesus.

This is precisely the point being made by *The Gospel of* Mary—it contains teachings that were unknown to Andrew, Peter, and even, one presumes, the rest of the Christian church that accepts the Gospels of Matthew, Mark, Luke, and John. This secret knowledge is something very different from the writings of the New Testament. It is portrayed this way because it is claiming superiority over the traditions in Matthew and the other Gospels that are revered by other Christians. It is a claim to truth. Indeed, it is a claim to *superior* truth. It is saying that those who accept *The Gospel of Mary* are better informed about truth than those who follow other Christian traditions.

Should we believe the Gnostic gospels or Matthew, Mark, Luke, and John?

Here is an important point for Christians: Which accounts of Jesus' teachings do we believe? Those found in Matthew, Mark, Luke, and John? Or those found in *The Gospel of Mary, The Gospel of Judas, The Gospel of Truth,* and others? And one has to choose—the two accounts are mutually exclusive; the teachings found in Matthew, Mark, Luke, and John are too different from those found in the Gnostic gospels.

One thing the character Teabing emphasizes about the Gnostic gospels is that they are the "earliest Christian records" (*The Da Vinci Code,* page 331); he goes so far as to describe them as "these unaltered gospels" (page 334). In one regard, Teabing is correct. One of the criteria that historians use when trying to determine the accuracy of one account over another is how close to the event were they written. The gospels written closest to the time of Jesus have the best claim for being the most accurate. But it is here that Teabing misreports the facts, because almost everyone who has studied them seriously believes that *The Gospel of Mary, The Gospel of Judas, The Gospel of Truth,* and the other Gnostic gospels were written much *later* than Matthew, Mark, Luke, and John.

Modern books include a publication date, but that is not true of documents from the ancient world. For example, although they give clues as to the date of the events they describe, none of the four Gospels in the New Testament explicitly state when they were actually written. As a result, scholars have to come up with the best estimate they can from what clues there are. The best clues are for the Gospel of Luke, because Luke wrote a companion volume to his Gospel—the book of Acts, which describes the history of the early church. The last half of Acts traces Paul's missionary activities and his eventual arrest by the Roman authorities. It finishes by describing Paul's arrival in Rome and his ability to continue to spread the good news about Jesus, despite the fact that he is under house arrest (see Acts 28:30, 31). From other chronological details given in Acts, this passage must have been written after A.D. 62.[16] If, as appears very likely, the Gospel of Luke was written about the same time as Acts, we have a way to estimate the earliest time that the Gospel of Luke could have been written. A wide variety of dates has been suggested, but the majority of scholarly opinion probably still places the writing of Luke-Acts, as well as Matthew and Mark, well before the end of the first century A.D., with John's Gospel being written toward the end of the first century.[17]

By way of contrast, the Nag Hammadi gospels probably come from a much later time period. Wesley Isenberg suggests that *The Gospel of Philip* was written in the second half of the third century (that is, somewhere between A.D. 250 and 299).[18] Some of the other nonbiblical gospels, such as *The Gospel of Mary* and *The Gospel of Judas,* were probably written earlier than this. Karen King and Jean-Yves Leloup date *The Gospel of Mary* early to mid second century,[19] while Marvin Meyer suggests a date mid second century for the *Gospel of Judas.*[20] So *The Gospel of Mary* and *The Gospel of Judas,* although written earlier than *The Gospel of Philip,* still come from a much later time period than those Gospels found in the New Testament. Thus, from just a consideration of the date of composition alone, Matthew, Mark, Luke, and John have the best claim to be an accurate report of the teachings of Jesus.

It is, indeed, true that the nonbiblical gospels, such as those found at Nag Hammadi, portray a Jesus who is different in many respects from the Jesus pictured in the biblical Gospels. But here is where historical judgment must be exercised. Which of these pictures of Jesus is most likely? As will emerge in the next chapter, although there was some debate whether certain books should appear in the New Testament, there was *never* debate about Matthew, Mark, Luke, and John. The early church had no doubt that Matthew, Mark, Luke, and John were "in," but that *The Gospel of Judas, The Gospel of Truth,* and other such gospels were "out"—"in" and "out" of the Bible that is.

Whether the early church chose the right gospels can best be answered by reading the other gospels that have survived and that were *not* included in the Bible—such as those found at Nag Hammadi. I, for one, after reading these other gospels, believe that the early church made the right decisions and that we should form our understanding of Jesus from Matthew, Mark, Luke, and John.

We are now in a position to comment on another of the key elements of the conspiracy theory advanced by Teabing and Langdon in *The Da Vinci Code:* the alleged role of Mary Magdalene. On the basis of our research and the evidence, we can say that it is unlikely that Jesus was married to Mary Magdalene, and highly unlikely that she was pregnant at the time of the Crucifixion and, thus, that she was the "chalice," or Holy Grail. Let's place this conclusion in our chart:

Constantine's "conspiracy" as alleged by the characters in *The Da Vinci Code*	
Claim by the "Royal Historian," Teabing:	True or False?
"Constantine . . . was a lifelong pagan who was baptized on his deathbed, too weak to protest" (p. 313).	Unlikely
"By fusing pagan symbols, dates, and rituals into the growing Christian tradition, he created a kind of hybrid religion that was acceptable to both parties" (p. 314).	
"Christianity honored the Jewish Sabbath of Saturday, but Constantine shifted it to coincide with the pagan's veneration day of the sun" (pp. 314, 315).	
"Until that moment in history [the Council of Nicaea], Jesus was viewed by His followers as a mortal prophet . . . a great and powerful man, but a man nonetheless. A mortal" (p. 315).	
"To rewrite the history books, Constantine knew he would need a bold stroke. From this sprang the most profound moment in Christian history. . . . Constantine commissioned and financed a new Bible, which omitted those gospels which spoke of Christ's human traits and embellished those gospels that made Him godlike" (pp. 316, 317).	
"Mary Magdalene was the Holy Vessel. She was the chalice that bore the royal bloodline of Jesus Christ. She was the womb that bore the lineage" (p. 336).	**Highly Unlikely**

The debate about what should and shouldn't be in the Bible cropped up toward the end of this chapter, and we will turn to this debate next.

CHAPTER 7

Did Constantine Decide What Should Be in the New Testament?

According the character Teabing in *The Da Vinci Code*, " 'to rewrite the history books, Constantine knew he would need a bold stroke. From this sprang the most profound moment in Christian history. . . . Constantine commissioned and financed a new Bible, which omitted those gospels which spoke of Christ's *human* traits and embellished those gospels that made Him godlike.' "[1]

How true is this? Did Constantine really decide what should go in the New Testament? Interestingly enough, while it is easy to answer this question—in fact Constantine did *not* decide what should go in the New Testament—it is much harder to answer the next obvious question: If Constantine did not decide what went into the New Testament, who did?

Jesus Himself spent His time preaching and teaching, yet no written documents from His hand have survived. Within a generation or so of His death, however, a number of documents were circulating in early Christianity. Among the first were letters from the apostle Paul, all written before Paul's death in the late 60s. The four Gospels, Matthew, Mark, Luke, and John, are also among the early Christian writings. As we pointed out in the previous chapter, it is usually thought that Mark was written in the late 60s of the first century, and Luke-Acts as well as Matthew are usually dated early in the last three decades of the first century, with John being written toward the end of that century.

The process by which these documents came to be regarded as Scripture is shrouded in mystery, although it appears quite likely that it was related to their use in the worship of the early Christian churches. Early Christian worship appears to have followed the practice of the Jewish synagogue in reading from the Old Testament writings as part of the worship service, understandably, since most early Christians were Jews. According to Luke 4:16, 17, Jesus Himself did this when He attended synagogue one Sabbath in His hometown, Nazareth. He first read from a scroll of the prophet Isaiah and then gave a short sermon about what He had just read.

After Jesus' death and resurrection, the practice emerged in Christian circles of reading from some Christian document, as well as from the Old Testament, in the worship service. Over a period of time, this practice would have the effect of elevating the importance of these Christian documents to a status similar to that of the Old Testament.

No evidence survives from nearly the first hundred years of Christianity of any discussion about which Christian documents were suitable to read as part of the churches' worship. But this changed when Marcion, a wealthy shipmaster, published a "canon," or list of approved books. Marcion, who arrived in Rome about A.D. 140, insisted that Christianity had superseded Judaism, so he rejected the entire Old Testament. In fact, according to Marcion, even some of the early Christian writings failed to recognize properly that Christianity had taken the place of Judaism; they needed careful editing, he said, to get rid of influences from the Old Testament. When Marcion published what he considered to be approved Christian writings, the document consisted of two parts: "The Gospel" (an edited version of Luke) and "The Apostle" (an edited version of Paul's letters).

Not surprisingly, Marcion's canon created considerable debate, and every so often for the next 250 years or more, some church leader would publish a list of books that he felt should be included in the New Testament—a "canon," if you will. It is astonishing to realize that it was not until A.D. 367—after the time of Constantine—that anyone published a canon that had exactly the same list of works that are found in the modern New Testament.[2]

This can be a bit misleading, however. It is important to note that from the first there was agreement on *most* of the books that should be in the New Testament canon. For example, there was never any debate as to whether to include Matthew, Mark, Luke, John, Acts, or the thirteen letters that name Paul as their author (Romans, 1 and 2 Corinthians, Galatians, Ephesians, Philippians, Colossians, 1 and 2 Thessalonians, 1 and 2 Timothy, Titus, and Philemon). Every list, except that of Marcion, included these writings.

Which books, then, were in question? Which nearly didn't make it into the New Testament? Hebrews was one, because nowhere does it say who wrote it. In the end, it was decided that Paul probably wrote it and that it should be included. There was much more debate about the book of Revelation. The fact that some extreme Christian groups used the book caused problems. Doubts about its authorship were raised as well, particularly in the Greek-speaking part of the Roman Empire. Revelation used language quite different from that of the Gospel of John, so, the question was asked, How could the same apostle write two such different works? In the end, though, Revelation was included. There was virtually no debate about some of the shorter works such as James, 1 and 2 Peter, 1, 2, and 3 John, and Jude, but sometimes one or more of these small books were omitted from a canon. Perhaps, it was an oversight because they were so short!

A few books *almost* made it into the New Testament canon but failed and are not included in the Bible today. Two, in particular, were considered by many early Christians to be good candidates. The first was *The Shepherd of Hermas,* an interesting book originating in Rome early in the second century A.D.; it contained many visions of the Christian prophet Hermas. The other book was *The Didache* ("The Teachings"), a book from the end of the first century or early second century A.D. It included what has been described as an early church manual as well as many good moral teachings. A less likely candidate was the so-called *Epistle of Barnabas,* but its claim to have been written by Barnabas, Paul's companion, was widely thought to be false. Curiously, little debate took place about *1 Enoch,* a book containing many prophetic visions, cited in the New Testament (Jude 14) and accepted into the Bible by the Christians in Ethiopia. However, there was little support for including any of these books in the New Testament canon—perhaps because, with the exception of 1 Enoch, they came from a time period *after* the letters of Paul and the writing of the Gospels.

But what about those "gospels which spoke of Christ's *human* traits" that the character Teabing says were deliberately left out of the New Testament by Emperor Constantine—gospels such as *The Gospel of Philip* and *The Gospel of Mary?* Yes, these gospels certainly do portray a different picture of Jesus, but it is a picture that most of the early church rejected because it was so different from that found in the earliest writings of Christianity, particularly the Gospels of Matthew, Mark, Luke, and John. Other gospels arose during the first few centuries of Christianity, but the point is this: No one seriously suggested that they should be included in the New Testament.

What about Constantine? Did he have any role in the formation of the New Testament? Not really, although he did make one important contribution. Diocletian (284–305), who reigned shortly before Constantine (313–337), had made a systematic attempt to stamp out Christianity. He destroyed not only many Christian places of worship but also as many of the important Christian writings as he could lay his hands on. So, by the time of Constantine, copies of the New Testament were in short supply. Several times during his reign, Constantine commissioned scholars to produce copies of the New Testament, including a number of copies destined for the many new Christian churches in Constantinople. Some of these have survived to be among the very earliest complete New Testaments that have come down to us from ancient times, although much earlier copies of shorter sections from the New Testament exist.

In one regard, then, *The Da Vinci Code* character Teabing is right. Constantine did, in fact, commission and finance new copies of the Bible. But—and it is a very important "but"—Constantine had *no influence* on what should or should not be included in the New Testament. By the time of Constantine, everyone agreed that Matthew, Mark, Luke, John, Acts, the thirteen named letters of Paul, Hebrews, and Revelation should be included in the New Testament. There was little residual doubt about the other books as well. So the character Teabing is quite wrong to suggest that Constantine deliberately left out certain gospels.

All this may be well and good. But did the early church make the right decision? What about the gospels that didn't make it into the canon, gospels such as *The Gospel of Mary, The Gospel of Philip, The Gospel of Thomas,* and *The Gospel of Truth?*

Ultimately, that question can be answered only by reading Matthew, Mark, Luke, and John—and then reading some of these other gospels. When I talk about what should or should not be in our Bibles I encourage my students to do exactly this. These nonbiblical gospels are readily available in English for those who want to read them and compare them with the biblical writings. *The Nag Hammadi Library in English* may be available in a conveniently located library and also includes *The Gospel of Mary.* These writings are also easily available in several locations on the Internet.

In many important ways, Christianity is the religion of a Book. Of course, it is *really* a religion centered around accepting Jesus as one's personal Savior, but we learn about Jesus from the Bible. This means that the Bible is particularly important to Christians and gives a cutting edge to the debate about which books should—or should not—be included in it. The kind of Jesus found in *The Gospel of Mary* and *The Gospel of Philip* is very different from the Jesus found in the Gospels of Matthew, Mark, Luke, and John.

If it were true that Constantine deliberately changed the nature of Christianity by the books he chose to include in the New Testament, this would have very great consequences for how we understand Christianity. The important thing, however, is that it is *not* true. Constantine did not change Christianity by choosing to leave out some writings and include others. With a few exceptions, the decision of what writings should be included in the New Testament had been made well before Constantine's time. *The Gospel of Mary, The Gospel of Philip, The Gospel of Thomas,* and *The Gospel of Truth* were written much later than were the Gospels of Matthew, Mark, Luke, and John, and there was never serious doubt in Christianity as a whole whether they should be included in the New Testament. It was clear to early Christians that they don't belong. They may shed interesting light on what some people were thinking about Jesus in the second, third, and fourth centuries,[3] but the most reliable picture of Jesus is the one found in the New Testament itself. We can have confidence in our Bible and in what it reveals about Jesus and His meaning for our lives. Furthermore, we can now put a comment next to yet another of the claims that make up Teabing's conspiracy theory:

Constantine's "conspiracy" as alleged by the characters in *The Da Vinci Code*	
Claim by the "Royal Historian," Teabing:	True or False?
"Constantine . . . was a lifelong pagan who was baptized on his deathbed, too weak to protest" (p. 313).	**Unlikely**
"By fusing pagan symbols, dates, and rituals into the growing Christian tradition, he created a kind of hybrid religion that was acceptable to both parties" (p. 314).	
"Christianity honored the Jewish Sabbath of Saturday, but Constantine shifted it to coincide with the pagan's veneration day of the sun" (pp. 314, 315).	

Claim by the "Royal Historian," Teabing:	True or False?
"Until that moment in history [the Council of Nicaea], Jesus was viewed by His followers as a mortal prophet . . . a great and powerful man, but a man nonetheless. A mortal" (p. 315).	
"To rewrite the history books, Constantine knew he would need a bold stroke. From this sprang the most profound moment in Christian history. . . . Constantine commissioned and financed a new Bible, which omitted those gospels which spoke of Christ's human traits and embellished those gospels that made Him godlike" (pp. 316, 317).	**Wrong. Although Constantine did commission a number of copies of the New Testament, he did not decide which works to include.**
"Mary Magdalene was the Holy Vessel. She was the chalice that bore the royal bloodline of Jesus Christ. She was the womb that bore the lineage" (p. 336).	**Highly Unlikely**

CHAPTER 8

Was Constantine the First to Say Jesus Was Divine?

We have seen that the character Teabing in *The Da Vinci Code* is wrong in stating that Constantine actively chose which documents to include in the New Testament. But what about his statements regarding Jesus' divinity? Teabing says that as one of the crucial steps in fusing pagan religion with Christianity, Constantine "held a famous ecumenical gathering known as the Council of Nicaea. . . .

"At this gathering . . . many aspects of Christianity were debated and voted upon—the date of Easter, the role of the bishops, the administration of sacraments, and, of course, the *divinity* of Jesus. . . .

"Until *that* moment in history, Jesus was viewed by His followers as a mortal prophet . . . a great and powerful man, but a *man* nonetheless. A mortal."[1]

Is this true? Did the followers of Jesus see Him only as a prophet, a man, a mortal? Was it only in the fourth century that Jesus was first recognized as divine? This and the following chapter will outline some of the evidence that this is not, in fact, true. What is true, however, is that the Council of Nicaea did make an important step in the way in which Christians understood Jesus. Let us begin by going back to the very first glimpses of what early Christians were thinking in the earliest documents of Christianity—to discover whether the first Christians really considered Jesus to be divine.

Paul and John clearly say Jesus is divine

Paul's letters are among the earliest surviving documents of Christianity. Paul certainly had no problem thinking of Jesus as divine. In Philippians 2:5–11 Paul says that although Jesus was in the

form of God, [he]
did not regard equality with God
as something to be exploited,
but emptied himself . . .
and became obedient to the point of death—
even death on a cross.
Therefore God also highly exalted him,
and gave him the name
that is above every name,
so that at the name of Jesus
every knee should bend,
in heaven and on earth and under the earth,
and every tongue should confess
that Jesus Christ is Lord.[2]

There is little hesitation here, as elsewhere in Paul's writings, to attribute to Jesus' equality with God.

The Gospel of John, like Paul's letters, also comes from the first century, and thus pre-dates the Council of Nicaea by at least two hundred years. There can be no doubt that John's Gospel portrays Jesus as fully divine. Take, for example, an incident recorded toward the end of the Gospel, when Thomas meets Jesus after the Resurrection. Jesus invites Thomas to put his fingers in the wounds of His hands. In response, Thomas falls to his knees and says, "My Lord and my God!" (John 20:28). In doing so Thomas is not only expressing his own belief but summarizing the picture of Jesus in the whole of John's Gospel. On the one hand, the Jesus of John is fully human. He gets tired on a journey (John 4:6), and He feels human emotions such as love and anger (John 11:3, 33). Yet the Gospel that shows Jesus at His most human is also the Gospel that most underlines His divinity. John is the only Gospel that records Jesus saying of Himself, "I and the Father are one" (John 10:30). For John, Jesus is the divine logos that came to earth in human flesh (John 1:1–14).

John records a number of sayings of Jesus that emphasize His unique status. Take, for example, the following statements that Jesus makes about Himself, all of which are found in the Gospel of John:

- "I am the way, and the truth, and the life. No one comes to the Father except through me" (John 14:6). In saying this, Jesus claims that He is *the only way to God.*

- "The Father judges no one but has given all judgment to the Son" (John 5:22). In saying this, Jesus claims that He is the *Judge of all humans.* Note that this is not a claim to be an earthly judge, but the much greater claim to be the One who judges all humankind at the end of the age.

- "Indeed, just as the Father raises the dead and gives them life, so also the Son gives life to whomever he wishes" (John 5:21). In saying this, Jesus makes the extraordinary claim that He has the *power to give life to the dead.*

- Jesus claims that He has *equality with God:* "I and the Father are one" (John 10:30).

- When Jesus said, "I am the bread of life" (John 6:35) or "I am the light of the world" (John 8:12), He was making the claim that He is as important to life as bread or light.

Matthew, Mark, and Luke clearly say Jesus is divine

The Jesus found in the Gospel of John, then, is both fully human and fully divine. There is no possible room for doubt about either His humanity or His divinity. Furthermore, the other Gospels are in agreement with this picture of Jesus. He is fully human. He lives and dies in a real country, and those with whom He interacts are historical persons. He hails from a town called Nazareth (Matthew 4:13; Mark 1:9). When He returns to His hometown with His disciples, He is known as the builder, the Son of Mary and the Brother of James, Joses, Judas, and Simon. He also has sisters (Mark 6:1–3). He begins His public ministry by being baptized in the river Jordan and then goes to Capernaum, where He makes His home (Matthew 4:13; Mark 2:1). He teaches and heals in the synagogue in Capernaum (Mark 1:21–27). His activities take Him around the Sea of Galilee (Mark 3:7; 5:1), to the regions of Tyre (Mark 7:24), to Caesarea Philippi (Mark 8:27), and finally to Jerusalem (Mark 11:1; Luke 9:51; 19:28–48), where He meets His death. He affects, and is heard by, a wide range of people, within and without Palestine, including such notables as Herod Antipas, tetrarch of Galilee and Peraea (Mark 6:14), and Pilate, procurator of Judea (Mark 15:2).

Jesus has a human mother and has human emotions. He is moved with compassion at the plight of a leper and reaches out His hand to touch him (Mark 1:41). He becomes angry at the hardness of heart that would lead the Pharisees to bring a cripple to the synagogue on Sabbath just to see if His compassion would cause Him to heal him on that day (Mark 3:5). He marvels at the unbelief of the people of His hometown (Mark 6:6). He has compassion on the hunger of the crowd (Mark 8:2). He looks upon the proud young man who can claim to have kept all of God's commandments, and He loves him (Mark 10:21). He becomes very distressed in Gethsemane as He contemplates the ordeal that awaits Him (Mark 14:33; Luke 22:39–46). He cries out in despair on the cross—despair because He feels forsaken by God (Mark 15:34).

The Jesus found in the Gospels of Matthew, Mark, and Luke is fully human. On the other hand, He is also divine. Others say that He is the Son of God. At His baptism the heavens open, and a heavenly voice says, "You are my Son, the Beloved; with you I am well pleased" (Matthew 3:17; Mark 1:11). The demons proclaim Jesus as the Holy One of God (Mark 1:24), and at the moment of His death the Roman centurion can recognize that Jesus is the Son of God (Mark 15:39).

Jesus does things no human can do. He heals the sick (Mark 1:29–34), cleanses lepers with a touch (Mark 1:40–43), and enables quadriplegics to walk (Mark 2:1–12). He restores withered limbs (Mark 3:1, 5), hearing to the deaf (Mark 7:32–35), and sight to the blind (Mark 8:22–25; 10:46–52). He can multiply five loaves and two fishes to feed a crowd of five thousand (Matthew 14:13–21; Mark 6:30–44; Luke 9:10–17; John 6:1–14). He walks on the water (Matthew 14:22–33; Mark 6:45–52; John 6:15–21). He raises the dead to life (Mark 5:35–43). He exercises authority over the spirit world. Although they are His enemies, demons recognize Him and obey Him (Mark 1:23–26; 5:2–14). He changes into a bright, shining being before the frightened eyes of three of His disciples and talks with Elijah and Moses (Mark 9:2–4).

This is no ordinary man. The Jesus of the Gospels is not just a mortal prophet: He is the Son of God.

Implications of what Jesus said about Himself

This observation raises the important question of how we should assess Jesus. Let me illustrate what I mean by sharing a family story. My wife, Susan, is now a hospital administrator, but she began her career as a nurse-midwife. At one point in her career she needed to upgrade her qualifications with a university degree. And this meant that not only would she have to take a number of academic studies, she would also have to spend time in a hospital specializing in psychologically disturbed patients, since up to that time her clinical experience had been confined to critical care hospitals.

During her experience in the psych ward (as she called it), Susan had lots of impressions and stories to share. After her first day, she came home complaining that a psych ward was a very disconcerting place because it wasn't always easy to know who were the patients! In the hospital environment she was used to, patients could be easily recognized; they were usually the people in pyjamas lying in beds. The staff were easy to recognize, as well. Nurses wore uniforms, and it was possible to tell from the uniform what experience and responsibility a nurse had. Doctors, too, were usually easy to identify— often from the way they dressed, and the stethoscope trailing out of their pockets or around their neck. But on a psych ward, patients, nurses, and doctors dressed pretty much alike. Beds were used only for sleeping at night; during the day it was hard to tell, just by looking at people, who were the patients and who were the health-care professionals.

Early in her time on the ward, she was invited to join a group session. As an icebreaker, those sitting in the circle were asked to describe what they would do with one million dollars. Because one man sitting in the circle was wearing a tie and looking very tidy, Susan had already tentatively classified him as probably one of the medical staff. When it came to his turn to speak, he confirmed this impression when he said, "What would I do with a million dollars? I think I would use it to get my books published." Being married to an academic (that's me), Susan thought to herself that indeed this might be an up-and-coming doctor trying to get some of his research published.

The neatly dressed person continued, "I've written a number of books, and for some reason publishing houses haven't accepted them for publication." Thinking about my experiences trying to interest publishers in my books, Susan then thought to herself, *Yes, from what Robert has been experiencing, it's not always easy to get research published.*

Then the neatly dressed person said, "You would think they would publish books written by the son of God!" Susan immediately decided he was a patient—not an up-and-coming doctor as she had thought. I can repeat this story and still preserve the anonymity of this particular patient because there is more than one person in a psychology hospital who thinks he is the son of God. In fact, it is a well-known psychological illness to claim to be the son of God or to be Elvis or to be Napoleon. Which leaves a very disturbing question: What about Jesus' claims to be the Son of God? This question has only a very few possible answers. Essentially, either Jesus was right about that, and He really is the Son of God, or He was completely delusional.

I always find this a sobering reality check. You see, as an academic, you learn to argue the strengths and weaknesses of several different positions. Many things that start out seemingly black or white turn out to be some shade of grey. The world is a complex place. Moral decisions are often difficult, not because one course of action is clearly right and another clearly wrong, but because there are pros and cons for each possible decision. Life is complex, and the moral decisions we make are complex. This is continually disconcerting, but one learns to live with the fact that many decisions in life—even important decisions—are ambiguous.

Yet there is little ambiguity when it comes to Jesus. He either is the Son of God or He was completely deluded. It is not possible to say that He was "more or less" the Son of God. That He was "perhaps" the Son of God. That He was "partially" the Son of God. Either He is God's Son or He is not. There is no middle ground.

Nor is this a decision that can be ignored. It has great potential consequence. Christianity claims that in Jesus, God became human and lived among humans subject to human limitations and conditions. It claims that Jesus' death and resurrection have changed historical realities. His resurrection is the basis on which we all can be raised to eternal life. His divinity gives Jesus the right to demand total commitment from His followers. When Jesus says, "Follow Me," as He does to every human, He does so because He is our Lord. His death and resurrection have provided forgiveness for our sins, and if we believe in Him, we have eternal life. This is an extraordinary, and confronting, claim. Either Jesus is the Son of God or He is not. If He is, then, at His name, every knee in heaven and on earth should bow, including ours.

When you think about it, this is a very confronting conclusion. In the way the Bible presents Jesus, there is no room for the kind of Jesus suggested by the character Teabing in *The Da Vinci Code*. Teabing says that Jesus is "a mortal prophet . . . a great and powerful man, but a *man* nonetheless. A mortal." That is a picture of Jesus that comfortably fits Him within historical processes. If it were true, we could then assess Him as a religious genius, just as we can think the same of Mahatma Gandhi or Buddha. This kind of Jesus might give guidance to our lives, but in a way that would be within the course of everyday experiences. The Jesus of the Bible, on the other hand, claims to be the Son of God, the turning point of history. If, in reality, He was merely a man, then He was deluded. But if He was indeed the Son of God, our decision to believe in Him is the biggest decision of our life. When He was here on earth, Jesus came to people going about their daily business and interrupted them by saying, "Come, follow Me." So, also today, He comes to us each one with the same challenge. "Come, follow Me." The Jesus described in the Bible is not just a man. He is the Son of God, who came to earth to die so that we might be saved from our sins.

CHAPTER 9

The Council of Nicaea and Constantine's Role in the Debate About Jesus

We have seen the evidence that the biblical Gospels—Matthew, Mark, Luke, and John—portray Jesus as both fully human and fully divine. That is the raw data, if you will, but it is hardly a carefully worked out theological statement of Jesus' nature. Indeed, one of the intellectual challenges that the early church had to deal with is this question: How can Jesus be both fully human and fully divine at the same time? This issue flared up several times before Constantine's day. Curiously enough, one of the earliest post–New Testament discussions on this topic questioned, not Jesus' divinity, but His humanity. We can find traces of this debate in the writings of Ignatius, an early church father.

Ignatius and Docetism

According to the church historian Eusebius, Ignatius was the third bishop of Antioch in Syria. He had run afoul of the Roman authorities and was condemned to be killed by wild animals in the amphitheater at Rome, where he died in A.D. 108. On his way to martyrdom, he wrote a number of letters to churches in Asia Minor that have survived. In his letter to the Trallians, he says

Be deaf therefore when anyone speaks to you apart from Jesus Christ, who was of the family of David, and Mary, who was truly born, both ate and drank, . . . was truly crucified and died . . . who was truly raised from the dead. . . . But if, as some affirm who are without God—that is, are unbelievers—his suffering was only a semblance (but it is they who are merely an semblance), why am I a prisoner, and why do I even long to fight with the beasts? [*Ign. Trall.* IX-X].[1]

In another letter—his letter to the Smyrnaeans—Ignatius also mentions "some unbelievers who say, that his [Jesus'] Passion was merely in semblance" (*Ign. Smyr.* II). We could wish that Ignatius had told us more about what these "unbelievers" were saying about Jesus, but he gives us enough clues for us to know that they were very uncomfortable with the human aspects of Jesus' nature. Ignatius says directly that they denied that Jesus actually suffered. His stress on the other human aspects of Jesus—that He "was truly born, both ate and drank, . . . was truly crucified and died"—might imply that these "unbelievers" also denied these aspects of Jesus' humanity. Thus, the likelihood is that these "unbelievers" were happy enough with Jesus' divine status but that they were very unhappy with the idea of His humanity.

Ignatius says that these "unbelievers" emphasized that Jesus only "appeared" (*dokeō,* Greek) to suffer. Thus, this belief has been named Docetism, and those in the early church who held this view have been called Docetist.

According to Irenaeus, Docetism was characteristic of many of the heretical Gnostic groups he describes. He includes an explanation of this concept in his general exposition of their ideas. Here is how he describes what "some" were saying about Jesus:

This Christ . . . descended upon him [Jesus] in the form of a dove at the time of his baptism, that Saviour who belonged to the Pleroma, and was formed by the combined efforts of all its inhabitants. . . . He also continued free from all suffering, since indeed it was not possible that He should suffer who was at once incomprehensible and invisible. And for this reason the Spirit of Christ, who had been placed within Him, was taken away when He was brought before Pilate [Irenaeus, *Adv. Haere.* I:VII].[2]

This full-blown Docetism is consistent with the general approach of the various Gnostic groups, which identified Jesus with one or other of the heavenly beings. In Gnostic thinking, Jesus appeared on earth to share secret knowledge about heavenly realities, not to suffer and die for sins. Thus, for them, the important heavenly aspect of Jesus was not present during the times during which He experienced the greatest changes—His birth and childhood or His suffering. Thus, for them, the heavenly being, "The Christ," joined Jesus only at His baptism and left Him before He died. Although we can't be certain that Ignatius is describing these Gnostic groups when he writes about these "unbelievers" that are troubling the church, his description certainly seems to fit with what we know of their beliefs. It seems likely, then, that the groups Ignatius attacks, as well as other Docetists who arose later, all had misgivings about the real humanity of Jesus. They were comfortable with the idea that He was a heavenly being but not that He was a man.

The Gospel of Philip and *The Gospel of Judas,* as well as the surviving fragments of *The Gospel of Mary,* do not explicitly state that Jesus only appeared to be human,[3] so we can't say that they reflect Docetism. On the other hand, they hardly stress the *earthly* aspects of Jesus' life, as Dan Brown has his character Teabing claim in *The Da Vinci Code.* If they stress anything, they stress Jesus' heavenly, or divine, nature.

The New Testament provides evidence that Jesus *was* accepted as fully divine in the first century. In the second century, even many of those labeled as heretics were emphasizing His divinity. Thus, it simply is not true to say that before the Council of Nicaea (A.D. 325) Jesus was viewed *only* as "a great and powerful man, but a *man* nonetheless. A mortal." Quite the contrary.

What, then, did the Council of Nicaea actually discuss regarding Jesus?

Arius

The Council of Nicaea did, in fact, devote considerable attention to a debate about Jesus' nature, and Teabing is correct to say that this discussion concerned Jesus' status as fully divine. What Teabing does not say, however, is that the debate took place in response to the ideas of an individual named Arius—*not* some suppressed gospels that emphasize Jesus' humanity.

As we have seen, the Docetists solved the problem of how Jesus could be both fully human and fully divine at the same time by downplaying His humanity and emphasizing the divine aspect of His nature. However, this was not the solution reached by every early Christian group. Some took the opposite approach—downplaying His divinity and emphasizing His humanity. Among these was a vociferous and influential group—the Arians—that was causing problems for some of the bishops who assembled at Nicaea. The Arians took their name from Arius and his ideas. Before we look at what happened at the Council, we should probably get a little background on Arius and his beliefs.

Arius was a presbyter, a priest, in Alexandria, Egypt. In one of his surviving letters he explains the starting point of his position: "We acknowledge One God, alone unbegotten, alone everlasting, alone unbegun, alone true, alone having immortality, alone wise, alone good, alone sovereign; judge, governor . . ."[4] In these words, one can begin to feel the persuasive power of this man, who, together with his followers, stressed God's uniqueness. This position, of course, leaves little room for a divine Jesus.

In addition, Arius skillfully promoted his ideas and was able to express his ideas in simple, easy-to-remember words. One of his slogans was "There was when he [Jesus] was not." These words summed up his essential understanding about Jesus' nature. In Arius's view, Jesus was the Firstborn of creation, and this meant that He had a beginning at some point. Arius also concluded that Jesus had no direct knowledge of His Father despite the fact that He was God's wisdom and Word.[5] These were the ideas that Arius published in his earliest confrontations with other church leaders over the nature of Jesus.[6]

Arius and followers were able to tap into a rich vein of biblical data to emphasize God's uniqueness. But in doing so, they also ignored other biblical evidence. For example, in the same Gospel in which Jesus says "The Father is greater than I" (John 14:28) he also says "The Father and I are one" (John 10:30).

It is hard to pinpoint exactly when the trouble began, but dissension grew until several clerics complained about Arius to his bishop. Arius was then summoned to a meeting of all the clergy of Alexandria, confronted with the complaints against his ideas, and urged to change his mind. He refused and was eventually excommunicated and banished from Alexandria. Things became even more complicated when bishops in other parts of the empire began to intervene. Some supported Arius; others denounced him. About this time, due to growing persecution of the church, Christians were forbidden to assemble, so the issues Arius had raised couldn't be solved; nothing decisive could be done.

During all this time, Arius and his followers proved to be masters of propaganda—even workers in the dockyards were singing songs about the controversy! At all levels of the church, the debate continued—sometimes with such an intensity that riots almost erupted. Such was the situation in the eastern half of the empire when Constantine finally seized control of that area.

Constantine and the Council of Nicaea

In his campaign to take over the eastern part of the Roman Empire, Constantine portrayed himself as the one who had rescued Christians from persecution. And as soon as he had control, he immediately set about restoring confiscated property to Christians and to Christian churches. Before long, the issue of Arius and his ideas came to the emperor's attention. When he couldn't get the parties to agree, he instructed that all church leaders from the eastern part of the empire, as well as many of the more important church officials from the western portion of the empire, should come together at Nicaea to decide several important matters that concerned the Christian church. To the best of our knowledge today, it seems that Constantine did take part in the debates at the Council of Nicaea; however, no matter what the issue, his contributions tended to try to move the council toward a solution that was acceptable to as many of the delegates as possible. The council dealt with a number of issues, but the controversy over Jesus' nature, which Arius's ideas had initiated, was the first item the council took up.

After some debate, the delegates agreed on a statement regarding Jesus' nature; today, we know this statement as the Nicene Creed. It is worth quoting here because it provides insight into the thinking of the church at the time—and it is evidence that Arius and his followers lost at the Council of Nicaea. The council rejected Arius's views on the nature of Jesus. Here, then, is the Nicene Creed:

We believe in One God, the Father, Almighty, Maker of all things visible and invisible:

And in One Lord Jesus Christ, the Son of God, begotten of the Father, Only-begotten, that is, from the substance of the Father; God from God, Light from Light, Very God from Very God, begotten, not made, consubstantial with the Father, by whom all things were made, both things in heaven and things in earth. Who for us men and for our salvation came down and was incarnate, was made man, suffered, and rose again the third day, ascended into heaven, and is coming to judge living and dead.

And in the Holy Ghost.

And those who say "There was when He was not," and "Before His generation He was not," and "He came to be from nothing," or those who pretend that the Son of God is "Of another *hypostasis* or substance," or "created," or "alterable," or "mutable," the Catholic and Apostolic Church anathematizes.[7]

Most of the ideas rejected (anathematized) in the final paragraph are those of Arius and his followers, and some of the language in the second paragraph, the paragraph dealing with Jesus, reflects statements that had been developed in dispute with Arius. The bishops assembled at Nicaea were all invited to sign the creed, and with only two exceptions, they all signed. Constantine exiled those two.

Was that the end of the story? Had they all agreed on how to describe Jesus' human and divine natures? By no means. But the Council of Nicaea marked a very significant step in the church's understanding of Jesus' nature; they came to a conclusion with which most Christians agree to this day. A very large representative body of the ancient Christian church agreed to the wording of the Nicene Creed, and it had Constantine's authority behind it. It is a milestone in the development of Christian theology.

So, in one respect the words of Dan Brown's character Teabing are true. The Council of Nicaea *did* discuss the divinity of Jesus, and it did emphasize that He was divine. But this in no way implies that the idea of Jesus' divinity was something new. From its earliest days, the Christian church recognized that Jesus was divine. Thus Teabing is just plain wrong when he says that "until *that* moment in history [the Council of Nicaea], Jesus was viewed by His followers as a mortal prophet . . . a great and powerful man, but a *man* nonetheless. A mortal." Jesus had been recognized as divine as early as there were Christian writings. This is particularly true even in the gospels that were *not* included the New Testament; in fact, these nonbiblical gospels tended to overemphasize Jesus' divine nature at the expense of His humanity.

It's true that there was fierce debate in the church at the time of the Council of Nicaea about whether Jesus was fully divine. But those who denied His divinity turned out to be a minority. Admittedly, there was much about the debate that was political, personal, and downright problematical, but it resulted in allowing Christians to better formulate their understanding of Jesus. In the end, the church went on record as believing that Jesus is both fully human and fully divine. This remains one of the central mysteries of Christianity.

We are now in a position to place a comment next to yet another of the items in the chart outlining Teabing's claims of a conspiracy:

Constantine's "conspiracy" as alleged by the characters in *The Da Vinci Code*	
Claim by the "Royal Historian," Teabing:	True or False?
"Constantine . . . was a lifelong pagan who was baptized on his deathbed, too weak to protest" (p. 313).	Unlikely
"By fusing pagan symbols, dates, and rituals into the growing Christian tradition, he created a kind of hybrid religion that was acceptable to both parties" (p. 314).	
"Christianity honored the Jewish Sabbath of Saturday, but Constantine shifted it to coincide with the pagan's veneration day of the sun" (pp. 314, 315).	
"Until that moment in history [the Council of Nicaea], Jesus was viewed by His followers as a mortal prophet . . . a great and powerful man, but a man nonetheless. A mortal" (p. 315).	Just plain wrong!

Claim by the "Royal Historian," Teabing:	True or False?
"To rewrite the history books, Constantine knew he would need a bold stroke. From this sprang the most profound moment in Christian history. . . . Constantine commissioned and financed a new Bible, which omitted those gospels which spoke of Christ's human traits and embellished those gospels that made Him godlike" (pp. 316, 317).	**Wrong. Although Constantine did commission a number of copies of the New Testament, he did not decide which works to include.**
"Mary Magdalene was the Holy Vessel. She was the chalice that bore the royal bloodline of Jesus Christ. She was the womb that bore the lineage" (p. 336).	**Highly Unlikely**

CHAPTER 10

Did Constantine Mix Paganism With Christianity and Change the Christian Day of Worship?

An important aspect of the conspiracy theory advanced by Teabing in *The Da Vinci Code* is his claim that Constantine changed Christianity into virtually a new religion. He tells Sophie, "By fusing pagan symbols, dates, and rituals into the growing Christian tradition, he [Constantine] created a kind of hybrid religion that was acceptable to both parties [i.e. both Christians and pagans]."[1] Teabing and Langdon give a number of examples of this fusion—the halos seen on icons of Christian saints are actually Egyptian sun disks; the symbols of the miter, the altar, and the Communion are taken from "pagan mystery religions," etc. Teabing goes on to say

"Even Christianity's weekly holy day was stolen from the pagans."

"What do you mean?"

"Originally," Langdon said, "Christianity honored the Jewish Sabbath of Saturday, but Constantine shifted it to coincide with the pagan's veneration day of the sun." He paused, grinning. "To this day, most churchgoers attend services on Sunday morning with no idea that they are there on account of the pagan sun god's weekly tribute—*Sun*day."[2]

81

The process that Teabing and Langdon describe is one that is familiar to most Christian missionaries. As Christianity is brought to a new culture and is expressed in a new language, the Christian missionary must try to convey the essential elements of Christianity using the symbols and language of the new culture. The only really effective way to do this is to find something familiar to those within that culture that can be used to illustrate Christian concepts.

An extreme example is recounted in the book *Peace Child*[3]—well known to a previous generation of Christians. The book recounts the adventures experienced by Christian missionary Don Richardson and his family while they worked with the Sawi people in Irian Jaya. At the time, the Sawi had had virtually no contact with westerners or Christians. To his horror, Richardson discovered that as he told the story of Jesus' betrayal and crucifixion, the tribe members looked upon Judas as the hero of the story! The missionaries were confronted with how to communicate Christianity to those who considered betrayal of a friend to be a virtue![4] In the end, their breakthrough came when they learned about a ceremony that the Sawi used to make peace between two warring tribes. A child was exchanged between the tribes as a guarantee of peace. The tribes even called this child a peace child. This was the image that the missionaries were able to use to explain the meaning of Jesus to these tribes who had previously seen Judas as the hero of the story.

This is but one example of the challenges of bringing Christianity into new cultures and expressing it in new languages. As Richardson explains, "Redemptive analogies, God's keys to man's cultures, are the New Testament approved approach to cross-cultural evangelism."[5] The challenge of finding suitable, culturally appropriate means of conveying the meaning of Christianity was a challenge that the early church faced. In this process, change is unavoidable.

Thus, Christianity changed and adapted as it moved from the Aramaic-speaking environment of Galilee into the cosmopolitan Greek-and-Latin-speaking cities of the Roman Empire. As Christianity became the dominant religion in a particular place, it took over, or replaced, existing religious symbols and practices. For example, if there had been regular religious processions to a pagan sacred place in a particular area, that procession and place was taken over by Christians and given a particularly Christian meaning. The Christians tore down the pagan temples and altars and built Christian churches over them. In this way, many prestigious Christian churches were built on sites that had had importance for other religions. This is even true of the Church of the Holy Sepulchre in Jerusalem, which Constantine's mother built over the supposed site of Jesus' crucifixion.

At the time, Christians saw this process simply as Christianity triumphing over paganism. Former pagan festivals, such as the one that took place on the shortest day of the year (usually December 25 or thereabouts), were given a Christian meaning. Thus the various sacrifices and ceremonies enacted on December 25 to ensure the return of warmer weather were transformed by Christians into celebrations of the birth of Jesus, the Redeemer of the world.

Christianity has changed in the past and will continue to change in the future to meet the different circumstances in which it finds itself. That is a given. But what is up for discussion—and what has been discussed at length by each generation as it seeks to make Christianity relevant to the new environment in which it finds itself—is this: What changes are legitimate? Which ones are not? Another way to ask this question is, Which changes actually alter something essential about Christianity? And which do not?

Even in New Testament times vigorous debate took place about which parts of Judaism were essential to Christianity. This question naturally arose since the first Christians were Jews who retained the Hebrew Scriptures as authoritative and thought of themselves as the true inheritors of the traditions found in them. A particularly sharp debate took place about whether one could be a Christian without being circumcised. After all, in the Hebrew Bible circumcision is an important sign of the covenant between God and His people. Paul's letter to the Galatians reflects how seriously he took this matter, and the first international gathering of important Christian leaders took place to discuss it. Acts 15 records that those gathered felt the Holy Spirit led them to the decision that circumcision should not be required of Gentiles joining the Christian movement. But Gentile converts to Christianity were asked to abstain from eating meat that had been strangled. This later provision was no doubt put in place to allow believers from both Jewish and non-Jewish backgrounds to eat together.[6]

As they struggle to communicate Christianity in a new language and culture, missionaries think long and hard about what is essential to Christianity and what is not. Given the accelerating rate of social change that is found in contemporary society, theology teachers, such as I, also think long and hard about how to communicate what is essential in Christianity to their students, who are growing up in a social and religious environment very different from the one in which we formed our own ideas.

We should probably not unthinkingly accept everything that came into early Christianity during the first centuries. At the time of the Protestant Reformation Martin Luther and others realized that some things had been incorporated into Christianity that did not belong there and that these things had changed it substantially from what it should have been. This realization was a powerful impetus to the Reformation.

Nevertheless, we should also understand that the pressures acting on early Christianity are similar to the pressures that act on the Christian church today. And we need to realize that we, too, are in danger of allowing Christian essentials to be changed.

In summary, then, Teabing and Langdon are more or less correct in noting some of the ways that Christianity took over pagan customs and gave them a Christian meaning. But they claim too much for Constantine's role, I think. Such things as the adoption of December 25 to celebrate Jesus' birth and the incorporation of many pagan religious symbols and practices into Christianity all took place more or less independently of Constantine. Constantine's patronage of Christianity might have accelerated and protected the process, but it is hard to portray his involvement as the deliberate invention of a new religion that was acceptable to pagan and Christian alike. Christians had shown themselves intolerant of some changes in their worship practices, so much so that many were prepared to die for their beliefs rather than worship what they considered to be pagan gods. So they clearly were not going to accept some things they identified as pagan. On the other hand, Christians, without Constantine's guidance, had already incorporated elements of pagan religious practices that they felt to be appropriate to Christianity's new status as the dominant religion in a region.

There is one area, though, in which it is possible that Constantine might have played a more significant role in this regard, and that is in the change of the day of worship from Saturday to Sunday. The next two chapters will look at some of the evidence that lies behind the change in the day of worship—and Constantine's contribution to that shift.

CHAPTER 11

Did the Day of Worship Change in New Testament Times?

It is clear that a change in the weekly day of worship has taken place between Jesus' time and today. Jesus and His first disciples were all Jews and thus worshiped regularly on the Sabbath, the seventh day of the week. Luke 4:16 says, "And he [Jesus] came to Nazareth, where he had been brought up; and he went to the synagogue, as his custom was, on the sabbath day" (RSV). According to this text, Jesus was in the habit of attending the synagogue for worship on the Sabbath. And this continued to be the practice of His earliest followers, even after His death and resurrection. Paul, for example, regularly attended synagogue worship on the Sabbath to argue for his convictions that Jesus was the Messiah (see Acts 13:14, 42–44; 16:13; 18:4).

It is equally clear that the majority of Christians today worship on Sunday, the first day of the week, not Saturday, the seventh day of the week. It is quite natural to ask when the change took place. This chapter will answer two questions: Did Jesus indicate that He expected the day of worship to change? And, Are there hints elsewhere in the New Testament that a change had begun to take place among early Christians regarding the day of worship?

The Sabbath and Jesus' healing activities

It is highly unlikely that the change of the day of worship took place during Jesus' earthly ministry. He gave no hint that He expected such a change, even though the Sabbath was a major issue of conflict between Himself and the Jewish religious authorities.

This conflict arose out of a difference between Jesus and the Pharisees regarding Jesus' ideas about how the Sabbath should be observed. The Gospels describe several examples of the controversy that arose between Jesus and the Jewish religious leaders concerning Jesus' Sabbath activities. Matthew 12:1–14 can serve as a sample, since the two incidents recorded there represent many of the issues found in the other accounts.

Matthew 12:1–8 recounts what happened when Jesus' disciples casually plucked ears of grain as they followed Jesus through the grain fields on the Sabbath. At issue was whether this was a proper activity for the Sabbath. This particular story is found in three of the Gospels (Matthew 12:1–8; Mark 2:23–28; Luke 6:1–5). Here is how it is reported in the Gospel of Matthew:

> At that time Jesus went through the grain fields on the sabbath; his disciples were hungry, and they began to pluck heads of grain and to eat. When the Pharisees saw it, they said to him, "Look, your disciples are doing what is not lawful to do on the sabbath." He said to them, "Have you not read what David did when he and his companions were hungry? He entered the house of God and ate the bread of the Presence, which it was not lawful for him or his companions to eat, but only for the priests. Or have you not read in the law that on the sabbath the priests in the temple break the sabbath and yet are guiltless? I tell you, something greater than the temple is here. But if you had known what this means, 'I desire mercy and not sacrifice,' you would not have condemned the guiltless. For the Son of Man is lord of the sabbath" (NRSV).

The Pharisees in the story don't specify why they consider the disciples' activities to be unlawful, but most likely they considered their actions to be work—something forbidden on the Sabbath. When the disciples plucked the grain, they would be reaping; when they rubbed the grain between their hands to get rid of the husks, they would be threshing; and when they blew the husks away, they would be winnowing—all tasks that later Rabbinic literature identified as categories of work forbidden on the Sabbath.[1] Jesus vigorously defended His disciples' actions. He first cited the example of David, who, because he was hungry, ate bread that he was not entitled to eat according to Jewish religious rules. Then Jesus noted that the priests in the temple actually do more work on the Sabbath than on other days and are guiltless. Jesus observed that for the disciples, someone greater than the temple is present (i.e., Jesus Himself). Finally, Jesus said, mercy dictated that the disciples should be able to eat if they were hungry. The disciples, Jesus concluded, are *guiltless!* He defended their actions to the religious leaders and insisted that they were not breaking any law regarding the Sabbath.[2]

The second incident in Matthew 12:1–14 concerns a healing. It is recounted in Matthew, Mark, and Luke immediately following the incident in the grain field. Here is how Matthew tells the story:

> He [Jesus] left that place and entered their synagogue; a man was there with a withered hand, and they [the religious leaders] asked him, "Is it lawful to cure on the sabbath?" so that they might accuse him. He said to them, "Suppose one of you has only one sheep and it falls into a pit on the sabbath; will you not lay hold of it and lift it out? How much more valuable is a human being than a sheep! So it is lawful to do good on the sabbath." Then he said to the man, "Stretch out your hand." He stretched it out, and it was restored, as sound as the other. But the Pharisees went out and conspired against him, how to destroy him (NRSV).

As far as we can tell, the Pharisees would have had no problem if Jesus had healed someone who was likely to die immediately—even though it was the Sabbath. Later Rabbinic sources are quite clear that if human life is at stake, anything necessary to save the life could be done, even activities otherwise forbidden on the Sabbath. But the man Jesus healed was not about to die. His hand was withered, but this was not a life-threatening problem. The man's condition was chronic, not critical. According to the Pharisees, then, Jesus should have asked the man to come back the next day. Indeed, they posed the question to Jesus about healing on the Sabbath specifically in order to trap Him into "breaking" the Sabbath. They deliberately provoked a confrontation.

Jesus asked the Pharisees what their behavior would be if they had a sheep that fell into a pit on Sabbath. He pointed out that they would usually rescue the sheep. If that was the case, Jesus asked, why should He not help a human, who is much more valuable than a sheep? Thereupon He healed the withered hand.

It is important to note that in all of this, "the question under debate" between Jesus and the Pharisees "is not *whether* the Sabbath should be observed, but about *how* it should be observed."[3] Although there are some exceptions,[4] most academics that write on the subject would agree with the conclusions expressed by Donald Carson, who, after examining the evidence of the four Gospels, says, "There is no hard evidence that Jesus Himself ever contravened any written precept of the Torah [the Law] concerning the Sabbath. . . . Some of the Sabbath controversies became springboards for messianic claims. . . . There is no hint anywhere in the ministry of Jesus that the first day of the week is to take on the character of the Sabbath and replace it."[5]

So, the change of the day of worship cannot be traced back to the time of Jesus' earthly ministry. But is there evidence elsewhere in the New Testament that a change in the day of worship had taken place or was in the process of taking place?

The Sabbath in the New Testament

The change in the day of worship is unlikely to have taken place during New Testament times, despite the fact that an Australian scholar, Stephen Llewelyn, has recently published an article in the prestigious journal *Novum Testamentum* that argues that it did.[6] Llewelyn bases his argument on three texts in the New Testament: 1 Corinthians 16:2, Acts 20:7, and Revelation 1:10.

In 1 Corinthians 16:1, 2, Paul urges his readers to start setting aside some money for a "collection for the saints" that he is organizing and that they should do so each week. He says, "Now concerning the collection for the saints: you should follow the directions I gave to the churches of Galatia. On the first day of every week, each of you is to put aside and save whatever extra you earn, so that collections need not be taken when I come" (NRSV). Llewelyn argues that the Greek phrase usually translated "each of you" need imply no more than an individual offering was to be contributed. He concludes, "As it is not a matter of making a collection at home, a collection in the context of Sunday worship is not ruled out."[7] Llewelyn then quotes a suggestion from an earlier scholar, Willy Rordorf, that whereas Sabbath might have marked the seven-day week cycle in Judaism, for Christians Sunday had apparently taken over this role.[8] Llewelyn then suggests that one might therefore conclude that 1 Corinthians 16:2 could be taken to "strongly indicate that a Sunday meeting may have been held at Corinth."[9]

I am not entirely convinced that the conclusion that a Sunday meeting at Corinth is a *possible* reading of 1 Corinthians 16:1, 2 means that Llewelyn has found evidence that "strongly indicates" a regular Sunday meeting. It seems much more likely to me that in 1 Corinthians 16:1, 2 Paul is urging his readers to consider their financial situation from the previous week. This makes sense, in fact, if the Christians at Corinth were observing Sabbath as a day free of work and financial considerations (i.e., as a day of worship). In that case, the first day of the week would be the natural time for them to review their finances from the previous week, a type of business activity that was totally unsuited to a day of worship. Furthermore, there is nothing in the text that suggests that Paul has in mind a public meeting of the community. He seems to be talking about each believer setting aside money individually, not an offering at a public meeting.

In his response to Llewelyn's article, also published in *Novum Testamentum*, Norman H. Young asks a further question. We know that there were Christians of both Jewish and non-Jewish backgrounds at Corinth (see 1 Corinthians 1:22) and that it appears likely that all the Christians were able to meet together in the one place (see 1 Corinthians 11:20). So if they met weekly, on what day would they likely meet? Young says, "Bauckham reminds us that all forms of early Christianity were Jewish. Given this continuity with Judaism and the way in which communities tenaciously adhere to their holy days, its seems inconceivable that Jewish Christians shifted their worship over to meet with their fellow Gentile Christians on Sunday without so much as a murmur of protest. On what theological or rational grounds would Paul have advocated a practice of worship that would have split the community?"[10] In other words, the strong supposition is that the Corinthian Christians were meeting together to worship on Sabbath, not Sunday.

The next text that Llewelyn examines is Acts 20:7, which reads, "On the first day of the week, when we met to break bread, Paul was holding a discussion with them; since he intended to leave the next day, he continued speaking until midnight." Llewelyn says, "It suffices for the purpose of this article to show that a meeting of believers occurred on the first day of the week."[11] The issue is a bit complicated, because according to Jewish custom, a day was measured between sunset and sunset. So, the seventh day (or Sabbath by Jewish reckoning) would have been counted from Friday sunset to Saturday sunset. Thus if Luke was using Jewish reckoning, the meeting would have begun Saturday evening and continued past midnight.

But sunset to sunset was not the only way to figure when a day began and ended. According to Roman reckoning, a day began at midnight. So if Luke were reckoning time according to the Roman system, then the meeting described in Acts 20:7 would have extended into Sunday evening. Just to complicate things further, Llewelyn also mentions the possibility that the Babylonian and Egyptian practice of reckoning days from sunrise to sunrise might need to be considered to be as a possibility. In the end, Llewelyn says that which system of time Luke may have used or his readers assumed is not important. What is important "was the author's clear intention that his reader believe that the meeting occurred on the first day of the week."[12]

I'm not sure, however, that this advances Llewelyn's case. He has shown that a meeting took place on the first day of the week, but there is nothing to imply that this was a regular occurrence. In fact, considering the short time that Paul had been with the believers (seven days, according to Acts 20:6), and that he was leaving them the next day, this may have been an exceptional one-time meeting that took place outside of their regular times of worship. Acts records the meeting because a young man, Eutychus, dozed off and fell from an upstairs window, and Paul had to miraculously restore him to life (Acts 20:9, 10). The mention of "breaking bread" in Acts 20:7, 11 could have been a reference to the celebration of the Lord's Supper, but this hardly indicates a weekly meeting, since at this time, it was not unknown for the early believers to celebrate the Lord's Supper daily (see Acts 2:46).

In his article Norman Young adds a further point. "Luke refers to the Sabbath twenty-six times in his writings . . . and not once does he provide an negative comment. . . . Luke's references to Jesus' custom of worshiping on the Sabbath and healing on the Sabbath (Luke 4:16; 6:6–11; 13:10–17; 14:1–6), inform largely Gentile Christian communities some 40 or 60 years after Jesus death *how*, not *whether*, to keep the Sabbath."[13]

Llewelyn admits that his third text, Revelation 1:10, is ambiguous. Revelation 1:10 reads, "I [John] was in the spirit on the Lord's day," and Llewelyn admits that the first unambiguous use of the expression "the Lord's day" to identify Sunday is to be dated about A.D. 150—about fifty years following the writing of Revelation. But then he says, "It would be overly pedantic to insist that it did not mean the same for this author also."[14]

Even granted that the term *Lord's day* meant Sunday in later times, it is still a bit difficult to establish that it had this meaning in the first century. After all, Jesus had proclaimed Himself "lord of the Sabbath" (Matthew 12:8; Mark 2:28; Luke 6:5), so it is possible that John the revelator might have intended Sabbath when he spoke of the "Lord's day." Some scholars have even suggested that Easter Sunday—a once-a-year event—might have been intended.[15]

Other early uses of the expression "the Lord's day," are also ambiguous.[16] It is indeed possible that Revelation 1:10 is a reference to Sunday. But it might also be a reference to the seventh-day Sabbath or to Easter. If one wishes to establish the earliest occurrence of a shift of the early Christian day of worship from Sabbath to Sunday, then one would look for unambiguous evidence, and Revelation 1:10 is anything but unambiguous. Nor are any of the other possible evidences that Llewelyn advances. In fact, in light of the observation by Norman Young—that early Christians naturally kept Sabbath as their day of worship, because of their Jewish backgrounds—it appears highly unlikely that any real move in the day of worship had started to take place in the time period during which the New Testament documents were written.

If that is the case, what is the earliest unambiguous reference to Sunday observance among Christians?

CHAPTER 12

Constantine's Role in the Change of the Day of Christian Worship

Constantine did play a role in the change of the Christian day of worship, but that does not mean that he, himself, instigated the change from the seventh-day Sabbath to Sunday, the first day of the week. This conclusion grows out of examining two sets of evidence. The first is the evidence that Sunday observance had begun as early as the second century. The second is Constantine's apparent motive for his Sunday legislation.

The earliest unambiguous reference to Sunday observance in the early Christian church

The earliest unambiguous reference to Sunday observance among early Christians is found in *The Epistle of Barnabas*.[1] The date of this pseudonymous work is unknown, but it is generally described as an early second-century work written in Alexandria. The unambiguous reference to Christians observing Sunday rather than the Sabbath is as follows: "Wherefore we also celebrate with gladness the eighth day in which Jesus also rose from the dead, and was made manifest, and ascended into Heaven" (*The Epistle of Barnabas*, XV.9).[2]

Granted, that sentence alone may not appear to be all that unambiguous. But in context it is. Chapter 15 of *The Epistle of Barnabas* deals with the Christian meaning of the Sabbath and is part of a series in which the author interprets many aspects of the Old Testament as a series of symbols pointing to Christianity. He discovers these "Christian" understandings of the Old Testament through a process called *allegorization*—or seeing different aspects of the Old Testament as symbols, or allegories, of something within Christianity. For example, he points to the instructions given in Numbers 19 regarding the offering of a heifer and then says, "Observe how plainly he [Moses] speaks to you. The calf is Jesus; the sinful men offering it are those who brought him to be slain" (*The Epistle of Barnabas* VIII.1–3). This is but one example of how *The Epistle of Barnabas* finds Christian meanings in the Old Testament. The scapegoat, for example, illustrates "the type of Jesus destined to suffer" (*The Epistle of Barnabas* VII.10), circumcision is explained as, "So then he circumcised our hearing in order that we should hear the word and believe" (*The Epistle of Barnabas* IX.3). Explanations are provided for the food laws (chapter X), the outstretched arms of Moses (they represented the cross; chapter XII), and the Sabbath (chapter XV).

In chapter XV, *The Epistle of Barnabas* notes that God created the world in six days and that "the day of the Lord shall be as a thousand years." This, together with the fact that "the present Sabbaths are not acceptable" to God is given as the reason that Christians "celebrate with gladness the eighth day in which Jesus also rose from the dead."

Although these quotations from *The Epistle of Barnabas* may not be entirely unambiguous referring to early Sunday observance by Christians, it does seem highly likely to me that the author is interpreting the weekly seventh-day Sabbath in terms of a weekly meeting of Christians that took place on Sunday.

However, there is absolutely no ambiguity in a reference by Justin Martyr to Sunday observance among Christians. Justin Martyr died in A.D. 165, and writing from Rome, he states

And on the day called Sunday, all who live in cities or in the country gather together to one place, and the memoirs of the apostles and the writing of the prophets are read, as long as time permits; then, when the reader has ceased, the president verbally instructs, and exhorts to the imitation of these good things. . . . But Sunday is the day on which we all hold our common assembly, because it is the first day on which God, having wrought a change in the darkness and matter, made the world; and Jesus Christ our Saviour on the same day rose from the dead [*Apology* 1: LXVII].[3]

Here, then, is clear evidence that Christians assembled each week on Sunday to hear the readings from the apostles and the prophets as well as an exhortation on the reading. No mention is made of any meeting taking place on the seventh-day Sabbath. So it appears likely that by the middle of the second century at Rome, the day of worship observed by Christians was Sunday, and Sunday alone.

Christians assembling together on both Sabbath and Sunday

The situation was different elsewhere in the empire, according to the fifth-century church historians Sozomen (c. A.D. 440) and Socrates Scholasticus (c. A.D. 439). Sozomen comments, "The people of Constantinople, and almost everywhere, assemble together on the Sabbath, as well as on the first day of the week, which custom is never observed at Rome or at Alexandria" (*Ecclesiastical History* VII: 19). And Socrates Scholasticus writes, "Almost all churches throughout the world celebrate sacred mysteries of the sabbath of every week, yet the Christians at Alexandria and at Rome, on account of some ancient tradition, do not do this" (*Ecclesiastical History* V 22).[4]

So, in most places throughout the Roman Empire in the fifth century, Christians were apparently assembling together on two separate days of the week: Saturday (the Sabbath) and Sunday. How soon the practice of worshiping on two days of the week grew up in Christianity is uncertain.[5] What is significant, though, is that for some reason Christians at Rome worshiped on only *one* day—Sunday. Nobody really knows the reason, but it has been suggested the Gentile Christians in Rome stopped observing the seventh-day Sabbath and started worshiping on Sunday in order to distinguish themselves from their fellow Jewish Christians, and that they did so quite early. Among the reasons that Gentile Christians might want to distance themselves from Jewish Christians in Rome are the fact that periodically one emperor or another would banish all Jews from Rome (for example, Claudius, see Acts 18:2) and the fact that a special tax was levied on Jews in Rome.[6] Very little direct evidence supports this suggestion, but it does provide a plausible explanation of the known facts.

Constantine's role in the change of the day of worship

Whatever the reason, the practice for Christians at Rome was to worship only on Sunday. Here is where Constantine does play an important role. On assuming power, Constantine immediately provided relief for Christians in the territories under his control. His father, Constantius, had already pursued a policy of softening the effects of Diocletian's harsh edicts against Christians; Constantine openly rejected the anti-Christian legal provisions still officially in force. He very quickly passed laws that enabled Christians and the Christian church to reclaim property that had been confiscated from them during Diocletian's persecution. Over time, Constantine adopted an increasingly pro-Christian stance, proclaiming many laws favoring Christians.

March 7, 321, while solidly established in power in the western Roman Empire, and three years before he added the eastern empire to his control, Constantine proclaimed the first of a series of laws that facilitated Christian worship. It reads

Let all judges and townspeople and occupations of all trades rest on the venerable day of the Sun; nevertheless, let those who are situated in the rural districts freely and with full liberty attend to the cultivation of the fields, because it frequently happens that no other day may be so fitting for ploughing grain and trenching vineyards, lest at the time the advantage of the moment granted by the provision of heaven be lost. Given on the Nones of March, Crispus and Constantine being consuls, each of them for the second time.[7]

Constantine's later career often focused on the eastern empire, particularly his new capital, which came to be known as Constantinople (known today as Istanbul), but he was based at Rome at the time he was making these laws. No doubt he took his lead from the Christians at Rome when he nominated Sunday as the day on which Christians were allowed to abstain from work so that they could attend worship services.[8] Did Constantine actually change the day of worship, as claimed by the character Teabing in *The Da Vinci Code*? Not really. The Christian community at Rome had in all likelihood been worshiping only on Sunday for at least a century and a half. But Constantine's laws did much to assist the spread of Sunday worship at the expense of worship on the seventh-day Sabbath. The large numbers of converts who came into the Christian church at this time, therefore, came into a situation in which it was natural to meet on Sunday rather than on Saturday.

Constantine's laws did not immediately end the practice of many Christians of meeting on both Sabbath and Sunday. Indeed, as late as the middle of the eleventh century, one of the issues of controversy between the Latin-speaking church based at Rome and the Greek-speaking eastern church was a dispute about whether fasting should be encouraged on the Sabbath day. The eastern church vigorously protested the idea of fasting on Sabbath. In one reply, the easterners were asked, "However, you [Greeks], if you do not judaize, tell (us) why you have something in common with the Jews in a similar observance of the Sabbath?"[9] It's true that this was an accusation made in the heat of theological conflict, but it was an accusation that must have had some basis in the practice of the Greek-speaking churches. Apparently they were still observing the seventh-day Sabbath in some form.

Over time, however, the net result of the official support of Sunday observance was that nearly all vestigial practices of Sabbath observance died out in the Christian church. Contemporary Christian denominations, such as the Seventh-day Adventists and Seventh-day Baptists, who worship on the seventh-day Sabbath (Saturday) tend to have developed this practice based on their reading of the Bible rather than on any links to earlier Sabbath-keeping practices.[10]

Thus, while Constantine did contribute significantly to this process of changing the day of worship from Saturday to Sunday, it is hardly fair to say that he actually deliberately made the change. Nor is it possible to lay at his feet the responsibility for Christians adopting pre-existing pagan festivals and holidays such as Christmas. These conclusions allow us to fill in the last two squares in our chart outlining Teabing's conspiracy theory, as can be seen in the next chapter.

CHAPTER 13

Is Christianity As We Know It the Result of a Conspiracy Going Back to Constantine?

It is true that the rule of Constantine the Great marked a significant watershed in Christian history. Christianity was different after Constantine than it was before him, and some of those differences must be attributed to Constantine's influence. Thus, by any measure, Constantine was a very important figure in Christian history.

His contributions took place at the crucial moment that Christianity emerged from the shadows to gather itself for the change from an occasionally persecuted minority to a religion on the way to becoming a triumphant majority in the Roman Empire.

As one reads the documents from the time period, it is clear that Christians fervently welcomed what they perceived to be Constantine's positive influence on the church. Nor should this be surprising. Prior to Constantine's arrival on the political scene, many Christians went about in fear for their very lives, just because they were Christians. Christianity had faced the might of the Roman state as it made a serious attempt to wipe out the church. Thus an emperor that ensured the survival, indeed the prosperity, of the church was more than welcome. Also welcome were Constantine's political skills. He found a divided church, and while he was not always successful, he certainly was able to bring about consensus on some very important issues, notably the divine nature of Jesus and a common date for Easter observance. His patronage also had an enormous influence on the growth of the church. Seen in this light, Constantine's role is benign.

On the other hand, reading these documents with the hindsight of subsequent history, one cannot but feel a chill in observing the close association between the church and the civil powers. Constantine was but the first of a long procession of able rulers who used the church for their own political ends. Secular political leaders have different goals than does an institution set up to worship God, and some political actions were taken in the name of religion which are quite rightly condemned today as unchristian. As absolute ruler—and remember that Constantine was the undisputed head of a military dictatorship that constantly enforced its will by waging war—Constantine sometimes acted to support decisions of the church that he approved. The two bishops who could not sign the Nicene Creed were exiled. Constantine passed a law against heretics, whom he addressed as "Ye haters and enemies of truth and life, in league with destruction!" The law was used to confiscate their places of assembly—in other words, their church buildings.[1] His failure to suppress the Donatists in Africa shows that Constantine was not entirely successful in his attempts to pick winners, but that is not the point. From Constantine's time onward, the mechanism of the powers of the state continued to be used in church disputes. In future times, losers of theological debates would find themselves burned at the stake. The principle of the separation of church and state, so fundamental to many modern societies, is a hard-won principle that had to wait more than a thousand years after Constantine, until after the traumas of the Protestant Reformation, and then after more than a subsequent century of bloodletting before gaining widespread acceptance. Today we have no problem conceiving of people of different religions living side by side in one country; many of us experience it as an everyday reality. But for centuries after Constantine, such a situation would have been inconceivable. This should not be blamed on Constantine. He was acting entirely as might have been expected of the first Christian emperor.

Constantine, then, is indeed very important in Christian history and influenced the shape of the subsequent Christian church in several important areas. Nevertheless, the influence that *The Da Vinci Code* attributes to him is probably far in excess of actual reality. We have seen the evidence of this in the previous chapters, and we can see it clearly in summary in the chart of Teabing's outline of Constantine's supposed conspiracy:

Constantine's "conspiracy" as alleged by the characters in *The Da Vinci Code*	
Claim by the "Royal Historian," Teabing:	True or False?
"Constantine . . . was a lifelong pagan who was baptized on his deathbed, too weak to protest" (p. 313).	**Unlikely**
"By fusing pagan symbols, dates, and rituals into the growing Christian tradition, he created a kind of hybrid religion that was acceptable to both parties" (p. 314).	**This process was already taking place, and it is probably unfair to attribute it just to Constantine**
"Christianity honored the Jewish Sabbath of Saturday, but Constantine shifted it to coincide with the pagan's veneration day of the sun" (pp. 314, 315).	**Just plain wrong!**
"Until that moment in history [the Council of Nicaea], Jesus was viewed by His followers as a mortal prophet . . . a great and powerful man, but a man nonetheless. A mortal" (p. 315).	**Unlikely**

Claim by the "Royal Historian," Teabing:	True or False?
"To rewrite the history books, Constantine knew he would need a bold stroke. From this sprang the most profound moment in Christian history. . . . Constantine commissioned and financed a new Bible, which omitted those gospels which spoke of Christ's human traits and embellished those gospels that made Him god-like" (pp. 316, 317).	**Wrong. Although Constantine did commission a number of copies of the New Testament, he did not decide which works to include.**
"Mary Magdalene was the Holy Vessel. She was the chalice that bore the royal bloodline of Jesus Christ. She was the womb that bore the lineage" (p. 336).	**Highly Unlikely**

The errors summarized in the chart above are not the only historical mistakes and errors of fact found in Dan Brown's *The Da Vinci Code,* as others have pointed out.[2] Apparently, one cannot catch a train to Lille from the Gare Saint-Lazare in Paris (French language editions of the book have corrected this mistake in chapter 35). Notwithstanding what Brown says in chapter 4, there are not 666 panes of glass in the controversial glass pyramid that forms the entrance to the Louvre. (I haven't counted them myself, so I'm just taking somebody else's word for this.) Nor, despite its enthusiastic adoption by Greek architects and renaissance painters such as Leonardo da Vinci, can the divine proportion, Phi (the ratio toward which the division of adjacent numbers in the Fibonacci series tends—approximately 1.618), be found when the distance between one's head and the floor is divided by the distance between one's navel and the floor. Nor is it found by dividing the distance between one's shoulder and fingertips by the distance between one's elbow and fingertips, even on beautiful people (see chapter 20). On the other hand, Phi *is* the ratio between the spirals on a sunflower seed as claimed in *The Da Vinci Code,* and, surprisingly enough, Phi is the ratio of actual descendents of male and female bees in a beehive, although not the ratio of the bees actually living in a hive at any one time. Other complaints about the book also circulate. Some of my colleagues from the arts faculty who have read *The Da Vinci Code* have even complained that it is poorly written! I have to confess that when I hear such a criticism, I often think to myself, *If only I could write that poorly. I would love to pay taxes on the royalties generated by the sales that* The Da Vinci Code *has enjoyed!*

On the other hand, many things in the book reflect historical and modern realities. The lines of longitude, which today use the line going through Greenwich, England, as the prime meridian (i.e., the line numbered zero), have not always been measured from Greenwich. The original prime meridian, the rose line, passed through Paris and is recorded in the floor of the Saint Sulpice church in Paris, as well as elsewhere (chapter 22). While the character Teabing is fictional, his supposed residence, the Château Villette, actually exists in the environs of Versailles and looks rather as it is described in chapter 52. Those who can afford it can actually rent the place. The street Rue Haxo exists, although it does not have a number 24, nor is it the address of the depository bank of Zurich (chapter 40).

I expect some of my readers at this point will be reacting a little as I did in a recent conversation with a colleague about the interpretation of the artwork presented in *The Da Vinci Code.* One of the advantages of working where I do is that the campus is small enough that most of the faculty know each other. Soon after reading *The Da Vinci Code,* I happened to be eating a meal with one of the art teachers, and we were comparing notes. I was complaining about some of the historical problems in the book. It didn't really surprise me that the art teacher had a different set of problems with the book—he thought some of the interpretations of the art provided in the book were quite inappropriate. What did surprise me was how strongly the art teacher felt about it. I remember thinking, *Hey, wait a minute! This is a work of fiction. We aren't expecting dispassionate, academically acceptable art appreciation. Some of these changes were necessary to make the story work.* Then, I must confess, I noticed the irony in my own vehemence about the historical issues raised by the book.

It is true that *The Da Vinci Code* is fiction. It is not an academic treatise and should not be held to the standards of academia.[3] In fact, you might ask why I have bothered to write this book about a conspiracy theory advanced by a *fictional* character, the "British Royal Historian" Teabing. (By the way, there is no such thing as a British Royal Historian, although there is an Astronomer Royal.) And that is a good question.

The answer is summed up for me by Bart Ehrman: "*The Da Vinci Code* has succeeded where professional historians have miserably failed: it has gotten people interested in a range of historical questions about early Christianity."[4] It is true. Academics have not been very successful in interesting people about the kinds of issues raised in *The Da Vinci Code,* but Dan Brown has been able to turn them into a blockbuster of a novel. For years I have been teaching my students about the Dead Sea Scrolls, Gnosticism, Greek philosophy, the Nag Hammadi library, and the like. Their reactions have ranged from tolerance to mild interest. But now, these topics are up to the minute. They are on everybody's lips. There is enough interest to warrant publishing a book about them, this book. In fact, many books. So I have to tip my hat to Dan Brown. He knows how to make history interesting. Constantine, the Nag Hammadi gospels, the Council of Nicaea, all are now topical as well as important.

This book you are reading has been written for those interested to know what influence Emperor Constantine really had on Christianity, and I hope it has served its purpose. In the end, though, what we think about Dan Brown's book is less important than what we think about the kinds of issues it raises. And these, in turn, are much less important than what we think of Jesus. If Christians are right, what we think about Jesus is a question of cosmic significance and great personal import.

Places to Go
for More Information

Readers who would like to know more about the topics touched on in this book have a range of good sources that can be consulted.

Of the books available on *The Da Vinci Code,* the one that I have found to be most useful was that of Bart D. Ehrman, *Truth and Fiction in "The Da Vinci Code"* (Oxford: University Press, 2004). Ehrman is a specialist in the writings of early Christianity and knows whereof he speaks. Among the more popular books that are available, I should mention a book written by a couple of fellow Australians, Grenville Kent and Philip Rodionoff, *The Da Vinci Decode: Is Christianity "The Greatest Cover-up in Human History"?* (Warburton, Vic.: Signs Publishing, 2006). Lisa Rogak's, *The Man Behind "The Da Vinci Code": The Unauthorized Biography of Dan Brown* (Melbourne: Scribe, 2005), provides a useful biography of Dan Brown himself.

There are a good number of excellent general introductions to early Christian history. The one by Laurie Guy, *Introducing Early Christianity* (Downers Grove, Ill.: InterVarsity, 2004) covers much of the essential ground in an accessible manner. Those interested in more substantial works about Constantine himself and the evidence for his Christian convictions or otherwise, would find the following works very helpful: Timothy D. Barnes, *Constantine and Eusebius* (Cambridge, Mass.: Harvard University Press, 1981); T. G. Elliott, *The Christianity of Constantine the Great* (Scranton, Pa.: University of Scranton Press, 1996); and Charles Matson Odahl, *Constantine and the Christian Empire* (London and New York: Routledge, 2004). Barnes provides an excellent summary of the very complex political environment of the time, and a well-documented coverage of much of Constantine's activities as they relate to Christianity. Elliott gives a useful updating of Barnes, as well as a useful alternate viewpoint at times, and good long quotations from original documents. Odahl gives a more extensive coverage of the political side. In a few places, Elliott's text cites brief paragraphs of original Latin, but English translations are provided in footnotes for these rare occurrences. All of these books, while technical, are well written, and I read them with pleasure.

By far the best introduction to the Nag Hammadi discoveries is that of James M. Robinson, ed., *The Nag Hammadi Library in English* (San Francisco: Harper & Row, 1977). It begins with a brief account of the actual discoveries, followed by an English translation of each of the documents together with a brief introduction to each. Although *The Gospel of Mary* was not found at Nag Hammadi, a translation of that gospel is also provided in Robinson. Two books deal specifically with *The Gospel of Mary*. That by Jean-Yves Leloup, *The Gospel of Mary Magdalene* (Rochester, Vt.: Inner Traditions, 2002), provides a look at the original Coptic text, plus a translation and a detailed commentary. Karen L. King's book, *The Gospel of Mary of Magdala: Jesus and the First Woman Apostle* (Santa Rosa, Calif.: Polebridge, 2003), provides a translation—in two columns where more than one copy of a passage is extant—and then looks at the overall implications of *The Gospel of Mary* for understanding early Christianity.

The recently published *The Gospel of Judas* is most easily accessible to English readers in Rodolphe Kasser, Marvin Meyer, and Gergor Wurst, eds., *The Gospel of Judas* (Washington, D.C.: National Geographic, 2006), which provides both a translation and several papers that consider various aspects of the gospel. James M. Robinson's book *The Secrets of Judas* (San Francisco: HarperSanFrancisco, 2006) provides some of the scholarly gossip behind the publication of *The Gospel of Judas.*

For a general introduction to Gnosticism, it is hard to do better than the excellent book by Elaine Pagels, *The Gnostic Gospels* (New York: Vintage, a Division of Random House, 1979), which is still in print. Karen L. King's *What is Gnosticism?* (Cambridge, Mass.: The Belknap Press of Harvard University Press, 2003) is written for a more academic audience but still provides a very useful introduction to both scholarship and issues surrounding Gnosticism. It is probably the best recent book to recommend on the subject, despite the fact that I disagree with some of her conclusions. It is hard to know whether to recommend her book before or after recommending Irenaeus's work, *Against Heresies*—they are both very useful. Book 1 of *Against Heresies* provides a general overview of what was happening in early Christianity, at least from the perspective of the orthodox church. Many libraries will have Alexander Roberts and James Donaldson, eds., *The Ante-Nicene Fathers* (Grand Rapids, Mich.: Eerdmans, [1885]), and volume 1 contains a translation of Irenaeus. Fred Lapham's *An Introduction to the New Testament Apocrypha* (London: Clark, 2003) also provides a broad overview of the important source documents and what might be described as a more traditional view of the influence of Gnosticism.

The development of the canon has long been a staple of introductions to the New Testament. There is an excellent overview in Werner Georg Kümmel, *Introduction to the New Testament* (London: SCM, 1975), pp. 475–502, for example. For a more recent and somewhat different perspective, see Bart D. Ehrman, *Lost Christianities: The Battles for Scripture and the Faiths We Never Knew* (Oxford: University Press, 2003), pp. 229–246.

The standard work on the change of the day of worship is still probably that of Samuele Bacchiocchi, *From Sabbath to Sunday: A Historical Investigation of the Rise of Sunday Observance in Early Christianity*

(Rome: Pontifical Gregorian Press, 1977). It is still hard to better Robert L. Odom's *Sabbath and Sunday in Early Christianity* (Washington, D.C.: Review & Herald®, 1977), as a source of English translations of virtually all the relevant texts up to the time of Constantine. Other more technical works are listed in the footnotes to the relevant chapters.

Of course, the question of which gospels should be included in the Bible is one that is best answered by reading the relevant gospels. So as well as reading the Nag Hammadi documents, I warmly recommend reading Matthew, Mark, Luke, and John. These are available in a wide range of Bible translations. Of course, I would recommend my own book on the Gospels to any interested reader: Robert K. McIver, *The Four Faces of Jesus* (Nampa, Idaho: Pacific Press®, 2000).

Notes

Chapter One: The Conspiracy

1. The figures are those found in a sidebar to the article "The Ways of *Opus Dei*" in *Time* magazine, April 24, 2006, page 28.

2. Nikki Finke, "Da Vinci Code Is 2nd Biggest Opening Weekend of All Time Worldwide," *Nikki Finke's Deadline Hollywood Weekly*, <www.deadlinehollywooddaily.com/first-bo-reports-on-da-vinci-code> (June 1, 2006). Numbers were boosted by strong attendances outside the United States. Within the United States, *The Da Vinci Code* movie actually ranked fourteenth for its opening weekend (just ahead of *Austin Powers in Goldmember* and behind *The Passion of the Christ* and *Star Wars: Episode II—Attack of the Clones*; see "Opening Weekends," *Box Office Mojo* <boxofficemojo.com./alltime/weekends> [June 1, 2006]). The movie *X-Men: The Last Stand*, which appeared in movie theatres one week later, had a bigger opening weekend than *The Da Vinci Code* (<news.yahoo.com/s/nm/=20060528/film-nm/leisure_boxoffice_dc> [1 June 2006]), so the record of second biggest worldwide opening weekend was held by *The Da Vinci Code* movie for exactly one week.

3. As of 11 July 2006, *The Da Vinci Code* movie had grossed $727,910,326, far outstripping other movies released in the first

six months of 2006, *Ice Age: The Meltdown* at twenty-eighth place (and $622,813,007) and *X-Men: The Last Stand* at fifty-ninth place (and $436,833,947). Interestingly enough, at gross receipts of $1,835,300,000, the 1997 movie *Titanic* is still the number one grossing movie, far ahead of second place, *The Lord of the Rings: The Return of the King* ($1,129,219,252; 2003), and third place holder, *Harry Potter and the Sorcerer's Stone* ($968,657,891; 2001). "All-Time Worldwide Boxoffice," *IMDb*, 11 July 2006, <www.imdb.com/boxoffice/allt imegross?region=world-wide> (12 July 2006).

4. The following citations from *The Da Vinci Code* are taken from chapters 55, 56, and 58. The page numbers throughout this book are those of the paperback edition. Dan Brown, *The Da Vinci Code* (London: Corgi, 2003).

5. Brown, *Da Vinci Code*, 312, 313.

6. Brown, *Da Vinci Code*, 314, 315.

7. Brown, *Da Vinci Code*, 316, 317.

8. Brown, *Da Vinci Code*, 326.

9. Brown, *Da Vinci Code*, 327.

10. "He [Dan Brown] has repeatedly maintained that he believes in everything he presented in *The Da Vinci Code*, including the fact that Jesus and Mary Magdalene were married. . . . In the very beginning of *The Da Vinci Code*, Dan Brown writes, 'All descriptions of artwork, architecture, documents, and secret rituals in this novel are accurate.' But interestingly enough, about two months after the release of *The Da Vinci Code*, Brown was starting to back away from this 'everything is factual' stance that essentially served as an open invitation to millions of offended Catholics and others to denounce the book. 'Ninety-nine percent of it is true,' he said in May 2003." Lisa Rogak, *The Man Behind "The Da Vinci Code": The Unauthorized Biography of Dan Brown* (Melbourne: Scribe, 2005), 114.

11. There are a considerable number of Christian responses to *The Da Vinci Code*. As examples, in addition to the more substantial treatment of Bart D. Ehrman in his books *Truth and Fiction in "The Da Vinci Code"* (Oxford: University Press, 2004) and *Peter, Paul and Mary Magdalene: The Followers of Jesus in History and Legend* (Oxford: University Press, 2006), one might mention the short books by Josh Mc-

Dowell, *The Quest for Answers: "The Da Vinci Code,"* imprint edition (Singapore: Campus Crusade Asia Limited, 2006); Lee Strobel and Gary Poole, *Exploring "The Da Vinci Code"* (Grand Rapids, Mich.: Zondervan, 2006); Hank Hanegraaff and Paul L. Maier, *"The Da Vinci Code": Fact or Fiction?* (Wheaton, Ill.: Tindale, 2004); Garry Williams, *"The Da Vinci Code": From Dan Brown's Fiction to Mary Magdalene's Faith* (Ross-shire, Scotland: Christian Focus, 2006); and Grenville Kent and Philip Rodionoff, *The Da Vinci Decode: Is Christianity "The Greatest Cover-up in Human History"?* (Warburton, Vic.: Signs, 2006).

12. Excerpts of the sermon made prime-time news coverage as far away as Australia. The text of the sermon can be read at <www.archbishopofcanterbury.org/sermons_speeches/060416a.htm> as of 19 July 2006.

Chapter Two: Who Was Constantine and Was He a Lifelong Pagan?

1. Dan Brown, *The Da Vinci Code* (London: Corgi, 2003), 313.

2. Timothy D. Barnes, *Constantine and Eusebius* (Cambridge, Mass.: Harvard University Press, 1981), 245, 246.

3. Barnes, *Constantine and Eusebius*, 346, 347.

4. See the discussion of Christian numbers at the beginning of the fourth century in Rodney Stark, *The Rise of Christianity* (San Francisco: HarperSanFrancisco, 1997), 5–7; and T. G. Elliott, *The Christianity of Constantine the Great* (Scranton, Pa.: University of Scranton Press, 1996), 13–16. Stark notes that his figures are consistent with a natural growth rate of Christianity of 40 percent per decade—a figure not that different from the growth rate that The Church of Jesus Christ of Latter-day Saints (Mormon Church) has maintained for the last century, and therefore, quite consistent with other measurable social phenomena.

5. Elliott, *Christianity of Constantine*, 25, 26.

6. Elliott, *Christianity of Constantine*, pp. 20, 21, certainly does so. Eusebius claims that he was a lifelong Christian. This is disputed by Charles Matson Odahl, *Constantine and the Christian Empire* (Lon-

don and New York: Routledge, 2004), e.g. footnote 9, p. 309. Odahl minimizes the possible Christian influence on Constantine before his conversion.

7. Elliott, *Christianity of Constantine*, 97–114.

8. Each of the emperors in the college of four set up by Diocletian had a special relationship with one of the gods: Diocletian was under the special protection of Jupiter; Maximian was under Hercules; while the junior emperors, the Caesars, were under Mars and *Sol Invictus* (the sun). (Barnes, *Constantine and Eusebius,* 11, 12.) Later, Constantine would be associated with *Sol Invictus,* a point noted by the character Teabing.

9. The concept that only a very limited number of repentances were available after baptism crops up in what is called the fifth vision in *Hermas.* In this vision, Hermas is given a number of mandates, or commands *(entolē)* by "a man glorious to look on, in the dress of a shepherd," whom Hermas describes as the "angel of repentance." The fourth mandate is a command to purity, which leads to a conversation about what one partner in a marriage should do if the other partner commits adultery. A husband who separates from his wife should not remarry, because she might repent: "It is necessary to receive the sinner who repents, but not often, for the servants of God have but one repentance." Still thinking through the command about purity, Hermas asks about repentance for sin after baptism: " 'I have heard, sir,' said I, 'from some teachers that there is no second repentance beyond the one given when we went down into the water and receive remission of our former sins.' He said to me, 'You have heard correctly, for that is so. For he who has received remission of sin ought never to sin again, but to live in purity.' " This rather intractable saying is modified by the possibility of one further repentance: "If a man be tempted by the devil and sin, he has one repentance, but if he sin and repent repeatedly it is unprofitable for such a man, for scarcely shall he live." *Shepherd* mandate 4.I.8, and 4.III.1–3, 6. The translations are those of Kirsopp Lake, *The Apostolic Fathers,* vol. 2 (Cambridge, Mass.: Harvard University Press, 1970), 69, 71, 79, 83, 85.

10. Brown, *Da Vinci Code,* 313.

Chapter Three: Real Life Murder, Mystery, and Mayhem: The Nag Hammadi Gospels

1. The discovery of the Nag Hammadi documents is recounted by James M. Robinson in two places: in his article "The Discovery of the Nag Hammadi Codices," *Biblical Archaeologist* 42/4 (Fall 1979) 206–224; and in the introduction to James M. Robinson, ed., *The Nag Hammadi Library in English* (San Francisco: Harper & Row, 1977), 21–25. Robinson cites his *Biblical Archaeologist* article in his discussion as to whether or not *The Gospel of Judas* is part of the Nag Hammadi library (he is convinced that it is not) in his book *The Secrets of Judas* (San Francisco: HarperSanFrancisco, 2006), 103, 104; thus, as far as Robinson is concerned, the account must still be accurate.

2. All of the translations of the Nag Hammadi documents cited in this book are taken from James M. Robinson, *The Nag Hammadi Library in English*. *The Gospel of Thomas* is found on pages 118–130.

3. As, for example, does Joachim Jeremias, *The Parables of Jesus* (London: SCM, 1972), 77–79, 149–151 [on the parable of the sower]. John Dominic Crossan, in his book *The Birth of Christianity* (San Francisco: HarperSanFrancisco, 1998), 103–120, concludes that Q—a lost source of Matthew and Luke—and *The Gospel of Thomas* represent the earliest written traditions about Jesus, and he bases much of his reconstruction on them.

4. Some Greek fragments of *The Gospel of Thomas* exist, which can be dated to A.D. 200, but even so, these are much later than the biblical Gospels, and there could have been significant development to the text of *The Gospel of Thomas* between that time and their publication in the form found at Nag Hammadi.

5. This assessment is also that of James D. G. Dunn: "But where *[The Gospel of]* Thomas differs markedly from the consensus of the Synoptic traditions in terms of particular motifs, the likelihood will usually be that the Synoptic Tradition is closer to the earliest remembered sayings of Jesus than is *The Gospel of Thomas*. . . . For while the question must always remain open that a particular *Thomas* saying has preserved

an early/earlier version of the saying than the Synoptic traditions or that an unparalleled *Thomas* saying is as early as the earliest Synoptic tradition, it will always be the undoubtedly early Synoptic tradition which provides the measure by which judgment is made on the point." *Jesus Remembered* (Grand Rapids, Mich.: Eerdmans, 2003), 165. On the appropriateness of the use of the terms *Gnostic* and *Gnosticism,* see the next chapter.

Chapter Four: The Gospel of Judas

1. This allegation is made by Gregor Wurst, who is cited in Andrew Cockburn's article "The Judas Gospel," *National Geographic* 209, no. 5 (May 2006): 95.

2. James M. Robinson, *The Secrets of Judas* (San Francisco: HarperSanFrancisco, 2006), 129–131; Robert Kasser, "The Story of Codex Tchacos and the Gospel of Judas," in Rodolphe Kasser, Marvin Meyer, and Gregor Wurst, eds., *The Gospel of Judas* (Washington, D.C.: National Geographic, 2006), 55, 56.

3. Kasser, "Story of Codex Tchacos," 61.

4. This and subsequent translations from the gospel are taken from Kasser, Meyer, and Wurst, *The Gospel of Judas.* The page numbers in parentheses give the page within this translation from which the citation is taken.

5. Bart D. Ehrman, "Christianity Turned on Its Head: The Alternative Vision of the Gospel of Judas," in Kasser, Meyer, and Wurst, *The Gospel of Judas,* p. 102.

Chapter Five: Gnosticism

1. The title "Refutation and Overthrow of Knowledge Falsely So-Called *[Elegchou kai anatropēs tēs pseudōnumou gnōseōs],"* is that given to the work in Eusebius, *Ecclesiastical History* V:VII.

2. The translation is that found in Alexander Roberts and James Donaldson, eds., *The Ante-Nicene Fathers, Volume 1* (Grand Rapids, Mich.: Eerdmans, [1885]), 315, 316 [book 1, preface].

3. Karen L. King, *What Is Gnosticism?* (Cambridge, Mass.: The Belknap Press of Harvard University Press, 2003), 7.

4. The table is derived from the comments comparing the two groups in King, *What Is Gnosticism?* pages 159–162.

5. Karen L. King, on pages 164–190 of *What Is Gnosticism?* describes the arguments of a number of such scholars. She answers her own question, "What will happen now to the category of Gnosticism?" with the observation: "In the end, I think the term 'Gnosticism' will most likely be abandoned, at least in its present usage." In several places in her book *The Gospel of Mary of Magdala: Jesus and the First Woman Apostle* (Santa Rosa, Calif.: Polebridge, 2003), for example, in pages 155–160, Karen King reveals her stance more clearly, where she argues that *The Gospel of Mary* is not Gnostic, because "There was no religion in antiquity called Gnosticism" (155). Michael Allen Williams, in his book *Rethinking "Gnosticism": An Argument for Dismantling a Dubious Category* (Princeton, N.J.: Princeton University Press, 1996), likewise argues that *Gnosticism* is used for so many different phenomena in early Christianity that the term is rather unhelpful.

6. A writer such as Fred Lapham uses the term freely. For example, he describes *The Gospel of Philip* as "broadly Gnostic," and *The Gospel of Mary* as beginning with a "Gnostic discourse." See *An Introduction to the New Testament Apocrypha* (London: Clark, 2003), 95, 162. The words of J. N. D. Kelly, written over twenty-five years ago, still sum up the position admirably: "To speak of Gnosticism as a movement is misleading, for that term suggests a concrete organization or church. There were, as we have seen, plenty of Gnostic teachers, each with his coterie of adherents, but there was no single Gnostic Church. On the other hand, it is clear that behind all the variegated Gnostic sects there lay a common stock of ideas which could fasten upon, adapt themselves to, and eventually transform any religious movement concerned to find an answer to the problems of existence, evil, and salvation." *Early Christian Doctrines* (New York: Harper & Row, 1978), 26. See also the very useful summary of ideas shared by many of the groups found within Gnosticism in Elaine Pagels, *The Gnostic Gospels* (New York: Vision, 1979).

Chapter Six: Mary Magdalene and the Gospels of Mary and Philip

1. Dan Brown, *The Da Vinci Code* (London: Corgi, 2003), 328, 329.

2. James M. Robinson, *The Nag Hammadi Library in English* (San Francisco: Harper & Row, 1977), 138.

3. Brown, *Da Vinci Code*, 331.

4. Robinson, *Nag Hammadi Library*, 138.

5. Bart D. Ehrman, *Truth and Fiction in "The Da Vinci Code"* (Oxford: University Press, 2004), 143, 144.

6. In *The Da Vinci Code*, the character Teabing turns this argument on its head. He insists that because "social decorum" of the time "forbade a man to be unmarried," if Jesus had not been married, one of the Gospels surely must have mentioned it. (Brown, *Da Vinci Code*, 330.)

7. Ehrman, *Truth and Fiction*, 153.

8. First published in 1962, the translations found in G. Vermes, *The Dead Sea Scrolls in English* 2d ed. (Harmondworth: Penguin, 1975), had already done for the Dead Sea Scrolls what Robinson's book did later for the Nag Hammadi library: It made available in English an easily accessible collection of the crucial documents. Thus, it is possible for the nonspecialist to read a translation of "The Community Rule," the basic rules by which the Qumran community governed itself. This rule envisages an entirely male-only community. While not stated, it is clearly implied that this was also a celibate community. In fact, one of the intriguing issues raised by the archaeology of the Qumran itself is the female skeletons found in some of the graves associated with the site—explanations include the possibility that these were cooks or that some families lived near the community in the very primitive desert conditions available.

9. This point is made by Bart Ehrman in two places: *Truth and Fiction*, 155–158; and *Peter, Paul and Mary Magdalene* (Oxford: University Press, 2006), 248–251.

10. Ehrman, *Peter, Paul and Mary*, 189.

11. For further discussion on the atypical attitude that Jesus expressed toward women, see Robert K. McIver, *The Four Faces of Jesus* (Nampa,

Idaho: Pacific Press® Publishing Association, 2000), 132–140.

12. Robinson, *Nag Hammadi Library*, 473.

13. Brown, *Da Vinci Code*, 333, 334.

14. Robinson, *Nag Hammadi Library*, 472.

15. Robinson, *Nag Hammadi Library*, 473.

16. Rainer Riesner argues that Paul arrived in Rome in the spring of A.D. 60, which if one adds the two years mentioned in Acts 28:30, gives the earliest possible date for the writing of Acts to be A.D. 62. *Paul's Early Period: Chronology, Mission Strategy, Theology* (Grand Rapids, Mich.: Eerdmans, 1998), 225–227, 322. Udo Schnelle, *Einleitung in das Neue Testament* 4th ed. (Göttingen: Vandenhoeck & Ruprecht, 2002), 45, gives A.D. 59 as the date for Paul's arrival in Rome, and other possible dates are canvassed in Riesner, *Paul's Early Period*, 3–28. There is general consensus that Paul arrived in Rome within a few years (plus or minus) of A.D. 60.

17. Most who work with the Synoptic Gospels would tend to use dates close to those suggested by Werner Georg Kümmel in his *Introduction to the New Testament* (London: SCM, 1975), 98, 120, 151, 246 of A.D. 64–70 for Mark, 80–100 for Matthew, 70–90 for Luke, and 90–100 for John; or those suggested by Schnelle in *Einleitung*, on pages 244, 266, 288, of shortly before or after A.D. 70 for Mark, about 90 for Matthew and Luke, and 100–110 for John.

18. In the introduction to his translation of *The Gospel of Philip* found in Robinson, *The Nag Hammadi Library*, 131.

19. Karen L. King, *The Gospel of Mary of Magdala: Jesus and the First Woman Apostle* (Santa Rosa, Calif.: Polebridge, 2003), 3; Jean-Yves Leloup, *The Gospel of Mary Magdalene* (Rochester, Vt.: Inner Traditions, 2002), 6.

20. Rodolphe Kasser, Marvin Meyer and Gregor Wurst, *The Gospel of Judas* (Washington, D.C.: National Geographic, 2006), 5.

Chapter Seven: Did Constantine Decide What Should Be in the New Testament?

1. Dan Brown, *The Da Vinci Code* (London: Corgi, 2003), 316, 317.

2. In his thirty-ninth Easter festival letter of A.D. 367, Athanasius became the first church father to list exactly the same twenty-seven works in his New Testament canon as that which is found in a modern New Testament.

3. Before reading the whole of *The Gospel of Judas,* but based on what he knew about it and his extensive knowledge of the other non-biblical gospels, James M. Robinson anticipated that "*The Gospel of Judas* will in all probability teach us a lot more about the Gnosticism of the second century than about the public ministry of Jesus, or sayings of Jesus, or Holy Week, or the like." Robinson, *Judas,* 78 (compare to similar conclusion on page 183). Such, I think, has proven to be the case, and is true of the other Gnostic gospels.

Chapter Eight: Was Constantine the First to Say Jesus Was Divine?

1. Dan Brown, *The Da Vinci Code* (London: Corgi, 2003), 315.

2. All Scripture citations are taken from the NRSV or the RSV.

Chapter Nine: The Council of Nicaea and Constantine's Role in the Debate About Jesus

1. The translation is that of Kirsopp Lake, found in the Loeb Edition of *The Apostolic Fathers* (Cambridge, Mass.: Harvard University, 1977), 211. The citation from Ignatius's letter to the Trallians is found on pages 253 and 255.

2. The translation is that found in Alexander Roberts and James Donaldson, eds., *The Ante-Nicene Fathers, Volume 1* (Grand Rapids, Mich.: Eerdmans, 1969 [1884]), 325.

3. A possible exception is the following sentence from *The Gospel of Judas*: "Often he [Jesus] did appear to his disciples as himself, but he was found among them as a child." The translators provide a footnote, in which they explain that there is a possibility that the word they translate as "child" might be translated "apparition," giving the translation, "he appeared among them as an apparition," although they think this is the less likely translation. Rodolphe Kasser, Marvin Meyer, and Gregor Wurst, eds., *The Gospel of Judas* (Washington, D.C.: National

Geographic, 2006), 21, fn. 7.

4. The citation is from a letter of Arius and his supporters to the Bishop of Alexandria, c. 320; the translation is that found in J. Stevenson, ed., *A New Eusebius,* rev. ed., (London: Society for Promoting Christian Knowledge, 1968), 346.

5. See J. N. D. Kelly, *Early Christian Doctrines,* rev. ed., (New York: Harper and Row, 1978), 227–229.

6. Elliott (*The Christianity of Constantine the Great* [Scranton, Pa.: University of Scranton Press, 1996], 145–162) documents that later in his career, Arius moved significantly from the position of his earliest writings; something his opponents in the church conveniently overlooked as they continued to attack his position.

7. The text is taken from J. Stevenson, ed., *A New Eusebius* (London: Society for Promoting Christian Knowledge, 1957), 366.

Chapter Ten: Did Constantine Mix Paganism With Christianity and Change the Christian Day of Worship?

1. Dan Brown, *The Da Vinci Code* (London: Corgi, 2003), 314.

2. Brown, *Da Vinci Code,* 314, 315.

3. Don Richardson, *Peace Child* 3d ed. (Ventura, Calif.: Regal, 1976).

4. "I expanded further on the life and ministry of Jesus, trying to establish His reality and relevance to their lives, but without apparent success. The Sawi were not accustomed to projecting their minds into culture and settings so forbiddingly dissimilar from their own. Only once did my presentation win a ringing response from them. I was describing Judas Iscariot's betrayal. . . . At the climax of the story, Maum whistled a birdcall of admiration. Kani and several others touched their fingertips to their chests in awe. Still other chuckled. At first I sat there confused. Then the realization broke through. *They were acclaiming Judas as the hero of the story. . . .* A feeling of coldness gripped my spine. I tried to protest. . . . But nothing I said would erase the gleam of savage enjoyment from their eyes." Richardson, *Peace Child,* 177, 178.

5. Richardson, *Peace Child,* 288.

Notes

6. So Jürgen Wehnert, *Die Reinheit des 'christlichen Gottesvolkes' aus Juden und Heiden* (Göttingen: Vandenhoeck & Ruprecht, 1997), 269; Ernst Haenchen, *The Acts of the Apostles* (Philadelphia, Pa.: Westminster, 1971) 449, 468–472; and F. F. Bruce, *New Testament History* (New York: Sadlier, 1969), 268–290. Adam H. Becker points to some interesting evidence that outside the Roman Empire, during sporadic persecutions in Babylon, Christians would be offered certain types of food which, if they refused to eat, would identify them as Christians. The specific issue appears to have been related to blood in the meat, and, consistent with Acts 15, these Christians refused to eat because the animals had been strangled. Adam H. Becker, "Beyond the Spatial and Temporal Lines: Questioning the 'Parting of the Ways' Outside the Roman Empire," in Adam H. Becker & Annette Yoshiko Reed, eds., *The Ways that Never Parted: Jews and Christians in Late Antiquity and the Early Middle Ages* (Tübingen: Mohr Siebeck, 2003), 380.

Chapter Eleven: Did the Day of Worship Change in New Testament Times?

1. *Mishnah Shabbath* 7:2 reads, "The main classes of work are forty save one: sowing, ploughing, reaping, binding sheaves, threshing, winnowing, cleansing crops, grinding, sifting, kneading, baking, shearing wool, . . . " The translation is that found in Herbert Danby, *The Mishnah* (Oxford: University Press, 1933), 106.

2. The comments on Matthew 12:1–8 given here have restricted themselves to a bare presentation suitable to make the point that during His ministry Jesus did not intend to abrogate the Sabbath through His or His disciples' actions. Much more could be said on this important passage. I have written a chapter on the topic called "Four Scary Things Jesus Said About the Sabbath" in *The Four Faces of Jesus* (Nampa, Idaho: Pacific Press® Publishing Association, 2000), 39–46, and have written a more academic treatment of it in "The Sabbath in the Gospel of Matthew: A Paradigm for Understanding the Law in Matthew?" *Andrews University Seminary Studies* 33 (1995): 231–243.

3. The conclusion is that of James D. G. Dunn, in *Jesus Remembered* (Grand Rapids, Mich.: Eerdmans, 2003), 568, 569.

4. For example, Willy Rordorf, in *Sunday: The History of the Day of Rest and Worship in the Earliest Centuries of the Christian Church* (London: SCM, 1968), 63, 65, 66, argues that "It is a misunderstanding to hold that Jesus did not attack the Sabbath commandment itself, but only the casuistical refinements of the Pharisees. . . . The people who were healed by Jesus on the Sabbath were suffering from unmistakable protracted illnesses and certainly not from acute ailments or infirmities. . . . If therefore Jesus in accordance with the unanimous testimony of the Gospel traditions purposely healed people on the Sabbath who were clearly not in acute distress, his deeds of healing were an offence and a provocation. . . . All these people who were healed could certainly have waited for their cure until the next day (cf. Mark 1.32ff.). Why, then, did Jesus heal them on the sabbath of all days? Surely, not *only* because of his compassionate love, but also with the express intention of showing that for him the sabbath commandment had no binding force." Samuele Bacchiocchi's book *From Sabbath to Sunday: A Historical Investigation of the Rise of Sunday Observance in Early Christianity* (Rome: Pontifical Gregorian Press, 1977) challenges many of the assumptions of Rordorf's book, and since its publication, few have argued that Jesus intended to abrogate the Sabbath.

5. D. A. Carson, "Jesus and the Sabbath in the Four Gospels," in D. A. Carson, ed., *From Sabbath to Lord's Day: A Biblical, Historical and Theological Investigation* (Grand Rapids, Mich.: Zondervan, 1982), 84, 85.

6. S. R. Llewelyn, "The Use of Sunday for Meetings of Believers in the New Testament," *Novum Testamentum* 43 (2001) 205–223.

7. Llewelyn, "Sunday," 209.

8. Rordorf, *Sunday*, 195, states, "The use in this passage of the Jewish designation of Sunday ('first day of the week') presupposes the observance of the seven-day Jewish week in the Gentile Christian churches, but these Gentile Christian churches no longer observed the Sabbath with which the Jewish week stood or fell. We did, therefore, earlier ask the question whether Sunday, instead of the Sabbath, had not perhaps become the pivotal point of the seven-day chronology."

9. Llewelyn, "Sunday," 210.

10. Norman H. Young, " 'The Use of Sunday for Meetings of Be-

lievers in the New Testament': A Response," *Novum Testamentum* 45 (2003): 116. At the time he wrote this article, Norm was a colleague of mine, teaching New Testament at Avondale College. He has since retired but still lives in the district. We both know Stephen Llewelyn from our participation in events of the society for the study of early Christianity at Macquarie University. The academic world sometimes has such unexpected connections.

11. Llewelyn, "Sunday," 210.

12. Llewelyn, "Sunday," 219.

13. Young, "Response," 119.

14. Llewelyn, "Sunday," 220.

15. See, e.g. C. W. Dugmore, "Lord's Day and Easter," in *Neotestamentica et Patristica* (Leiden: Brill, 1962), 273–281; Kenneth A. Strand, "Another Look at 'Lord's Day' in the Early Church and in Rev. 1:10," *New Testament Studies* 13 (1966–1967): 174-181.

16. There is a reference to the "Lord's day" in *Didache* XIV, which says, "On the Lord's Day of the Lord come together, break bread and hold Eucharist" (Kirsopp Lake, *Apostolic Fathers Volume 1* [Cambridge: Mass: Harvard University Press, 1977], 331). But no information is given about which particular day it is; nor, let it be said, whether a weekly occurrence is meant, although that appears the likely meaning. The other ambiguous reference, found in Ignatius's letter to the Magnesians, is translated by Kirsopp Lake in the following manner: "If then they who walked in ancient customs came to a new hope, no longer living for the Sabbath, but for the Lord's Day, in which also our life sprang up through him and his death . . ." By this reading, Ignatius may be indicating that the community to which he writes has made the move from worshiping on Sabbath to worshiping on Sunday. If so, this would be one of the very early evidences for such a shift. But a closer look at both the original Greek text and some manuscript evidence show that while this is a possible reading, it may, in fact, not be the most likely reading. Literally, the crucial phrase in the Greek text reads, "no longer sabbatizing, but living according to the Lord's [life]" (*mēketi sabbatizontes, alla kata kuriakēn [zōēn] zōntes*). The only existing Greek text has the phrase "Lord's life," but most translators, including Kirsopp Lake, follow the Latin text which omits "life," and

add the word "day." See R. J. Bauckham, "The Lord's Day," in D. A. Carson, ed., *From Sabbath to Lord's Day: A Biblical, Historical and Theological Investigation* (Grand Rapids, Mich.: Zondervan, 1982), 228; see also Fritz Guy, " 'The Lord's Day' in the Letter of Ignatius to the Magnesians," *Andrews University Seminary Studies* 2 (1964): 1–17. Bauckham (224) lists no fewer than twenty-four separate nouns that follow after "Lord's" in one of the second century writers (Clement of Alexandria), who speaks of Lord's teachings, power, commandments, head, people, word, words, house, voice, etc. While "Lord's day" might balance the reference to "sabbatizing," it is not the only possibility. Indeed, as the Greek manuscript says "Lord's life," this has to be the preferable translation. If that is the case, "sabbatizing" might be a reference to living too rigidly according to the Jewish laws, rather as Paul asks "If you, though a Jew, live like a Gentile, and not like a Jew, how can you compel the Gentiles to live like Jews" (literally: how can you compel Gentiles to "Judaize"?—Greek, *Ioudaïzein*).

Chapter Twelve: Constantine's Role in the Change of the Day of Christian Worship

1. William H. Shea, "The Sabbath in the Epistle of Barnabas," *Andrews Seminary Studies* 4 (1966): 149. In his study "Aspects of Early Christian and Jewish Worship: Pliny and the *Keryma Petrou*" in M. J. Wilkins and T. Paige, eds., *Worship, Theology and Ministry in the Early Church* (Sheffield: JSOT, 1992), 88–90, Graham N. Stanton argues that the letter of Pliny to Trajan written in A.D. 111–112 is also a very early reference to Sunday observance. In his duties as governor of Pontus and Bithynia, Pliny had occasion to investigate Christianity. He discovered, among other things, that Christians "asserted that this had been the sum total of their guilt or error, namely that on a fixed day *(stato die)* it was their custom to meet before dawn, to sing a hymn by turns (i.e., antiphonally) to Christ as to a god" (p. 85). Stanton argues that the language "on a fixed day" implies Sunday rather than Sabbath. Such is possible, but surely the most that can be derived from this reference with any certainty is that Christians met together once

a week. The exact day is unspecified, so this text cannot be taken as an unequivocal reference to Sunday observance.

2. Kirsopp Lake, *Apostolic Fathers Volume 1* (Cambridge: Mass: Harvard University Press, 1977) 379.

3. The translation is that found in Alexander Roberts and James Donaldson, eds., *Ante-Nicene Fathers, Volume 1* (Grand Rapids, Mich.: Eerdmans, [1885]), 186.

4. These two quotations are most conveniently found in Samuele Bacchiocchi, *From Sabbath to Sunday* (Rome: Pontifical Gregorian Press, 1977), 196, 197.

5. Some evidence suggests that a weekly observance of Sunday was preceded by a yearly observance of Easter Sunday, although it must be admitted the evidence is suggestive, not decisive. See Lawrence T. Geraty, "The Pascha and the Origin of Sunday Observance," *Andrews University Seminary Studies* 3 (1965): 85–96.

6. This is the thesis Samuele Bacchiocchi gives in *From Sabbath to Sunday,* for example, on pages 165–212. After documenting the hostility to the Jews found at Rome, including second-century Christians at Rome, Bacchiocchi concludes, "Such circumstances invited Christians to develop a new identity, not only characterized by a negative attitude towards Jews, but also by the substitution of characteristic Jewish religious customs for new ones" (183). He further concludes, "The Church of Rome, whose members, mostly of pagan extraction, experienced a break from the Jews earlier than in the East and where the unpopularity of the Jews was particularly great, appears to have played a leading role in inducing the adoption of Sunday observance" (212).

7. Constantine's laws allowing Christians to worship are most easily accessible in Robert L. Odom, *Sabbath and Sunday in Early Christianity* (Washington, D.C.: Review and Herald® Publishing Association, 1977). The citation is found on page 255. A second law, promulgated on July 3, 321, allowed the manumission (freeing) of slaves on a Sunday.

8. There is an interesting historical footnote, here, in that the issue of who changed the day of worship from Sabbath to Sunday, and when, was one of the items of debate between Protestants and Catholics that arose during the time of Luther and continued with some heat up to

the time of Vatican II. The following comments from *The Catechism Simply Explained* by Canon Cafferata might be taken as representative of the style of argumentation. Cafferata says, "The Jews' Sabbath Day was Saturday; we Christians keep Sunday holy. The Church, by the power our Lord gave her, changed the observance of Saturday to Sunday. A word about Sunday. God said, 'Remember that thou keep holy the Sabbath Day.' The Sabbath was Saturday, not Sunday; why, then, do we keep Sunday holy instead of Saturday? The Church altered the observance of the Sabbath to the observance of Sunday in commemoration of our Lord having risen form the dead on Easter Sunday, and of the Holy Ghost having descended upon the apostles on Whit Sunday. Protestants who say that they go by the Bible and the Bible only, and that they do not believe anything that is not in the Bible, must be rather puzzled by the keeping of Sunday when God distinctly said, 'Keep holy the *Sabbath Day.*' The word Sunday does not come anywhere in the Bible, so, without knowing it, they are obeying the authority of the Catholic Church" (Canon Cafferata, *The Catechism Simply Explained* [London: Burns & Oates, 1947], 89). This catechism was first published in 1922 and either reprinted or revised in 1924, 1927, 1930, 1932, 1933, 1937, 1938, 1940, 1942, 1943, 1946, and 1947. The later 1957 edition takes a more conciliatory approach on page 89: "The Jew's Sabbath, or Day of Rest, was Saturday, kept sacred because God at the creation rested on the seventh day and because they wished thus to commemorate their deliverance from Egypt. The Church, using the power our Lord gave her, altered the observance of the Sabbath to the observance of Sunday, to commemorate our Lord's resurrection on Easter Sunday and the descent of the Holy Ghost on Whitsunday. There is evidence in the New Testament (Acts 20:7; 1 Corinthians 16:2) that the apostles were beginning to observe Sunday as a day of worship as well as Saturday, but the apostles made no law on the matter, and the full transfer from Saturday to Sunday was a gradual process, under the authority of the Church. Those Christians who believe in the Bible and the Bible only must have some difficulty in explaining why they keep Sunday holy and not the Sabbath." Catechisms written since Vatican II Council omit this kind of rhetoric altogether.

    9. R. L. Odom, "The Sabbath in the Great Schism of A.D. 1054,"

Andrews Seminary Studies 1 (1963): 74–80. The citation, part of Cardinal Hubert's treatise *Adversus Calumnias Graecorum* (Against the calumnies of the Greeks) is found on page 78.

10. Accounts of how Sabbath observance was adopted by the ex-Millerites who formed the nucleus of the later Seventh-day Adventist Church may be found in P. Gerard Damsteegt, *Foundations of Seventh-day Adventist Message and Mission* (Grand Rapids, Mich.: Eerdmans, 1977), 135–146; and Richard W. Schwarz and Floyd Greenleaf, *Light Bearers: A History of the Seventh-day Adventist Church*, rev. ed. (Nampa, Idaho: Pacific Press® Publishing Association, 2000), 56–58, 65, 66.

Chapter Thirteen: Is Christianity As We Know It the Result of a Conspiracy Going Back to Constantine?

1. This law is cited in full in T. G. Elliott, *Christianity of Constantine* (Scranton, Pa.: University of Scranton Press, 1996), 138–140.

2. The information in the next couple of paragraphs about errors and incorrect representations of historical realities in *The Da Vinci Code* comes from a variety of sources, including several Australian-only television programs. The information on the divine proportion Phi, for example, formed a segment in the science show *Quantum* aired on ABC on July 20, 2006, just four days before this book manuscript was finished. Other information is derived from a travel show aired earlier in 2006 that looked at destinations related to the book.

3. Nor should academics consider themselves above making mistakes. Further research often leads academics to change their minds about something they might have published at an earlier stage of their careers. Indeed, the further research I have done for this book has led me to wish that I had phrased quite differently one of the sentences in an article published earlier this year, and I probably would have nuanced a couple of other sentences in that article as well. (No, I'm not going to point out which sentence it is either!) One should not crow too much about mistakes in other peoples writings!

4. Bart D. Ehrman, *Truth and Fiction in "The Da Vinci Code"* (Oxford: University Press, 2004), 189.

IF YOU FOUND THIS BOOK INSPIRING AND THOUGHT-PROVOKING, YOU WILL WANT TO READ THESE AS WELL.

Searching for the God of Grace

Stuart Tyner explores God's perfect gift as revealed in the plan of salvation, the pages of history, and the principles of God's character. He takes the reader on a journey to find out how and why some religious people, including some of our parents, teachers, pastors, church leaders, and, perhaps, we ourselves, have gotten off the gospel path and tried to find a different way to heaven.

Paperback, 304 pages.   0-8163-2152-3   US$17.99

Salvation 101—Christianity Made Simple

E. Lonnie Melashenko

In this book Lonnie Melashenko, director-speaker for the *Voice of Prophecy* radio broadcast, helps you put aside creeds, the sordid acts of professed Christians, and denominational disputes, and takes you right to the core, right to the heart of Christianity—Jesus Christ and what He offers. Come explore the bottom line of our faith. In Him is our hope and encouragement. In Him is life eternal.

Paperback, 96 pages.   0-8163-2168-X   US$9.99

See With New Eyes

Ty Gibson

Thousands have turned away from God because of what they've seen in the lives of church members. They've been looking in the wrong place. Ty Gibson uses striking language and illustrations to lead the disillusioned and the discouraged to a new vision of God that will change their hearts and their relationships with people around them.

Paperback, 160 pages.   0-8163-1786-0   US$11.99

Order from your ABC by calling **1-800-765-6955,** or get online and shop our virtual store at **<www.adventistbookcenter.com>.**
- Read a chapter from your favorite book
- Order online
- Sign up for email notices on new products

Prices subject to change without notice.